ANNE WILLAN'S
LOOK&COOK
Italian Country Cooking

ANNE WILLAN'S
LOOK&COOK
Italian Country Cooking

DORLING KINDERSLEY
LONDON • NEW YORK • STUTTGART

A DORLING KINDERSLEY BOOK

Created and Produced by
CARROLL & BROWN LIMITED
5 Lonsdale Road
London NW6 6RA

Editorial Director Jeni Wright
Editors Norma MacMillan
Jennifer Feller
Editorial Assistant Julia Alcock

Art Editor Vicky Zentner
Designers Lucy De Rosa
Alan Watt
Production Editor Wendy Rogers

First American Edition, 1993
10 9 8 7 6 5 4 3 2 1

Published in the United States by
Dorling Kindersley Inc., 232 Madison Avenue
New York, New York 10016

Willan, Anne.
  Italian country cooking / by Anne Willan. – 1st American ed.
    p. cm. – (Look and cook)
  Includes index.
  ISBN 1–56458–192–6
  1. Cookery, Italian. I. Title. II. Series: Willan, Anne.
Look and cook.
TX723.W55 1993
641.5945–dc20   92–54485
                                                          CIP

Reproduced by Colourscan, Singapore
Printed and bound in Italy by A. Mondadori, Verona

CONTENTS

ITALIAN COUNTRY COOKING

THE LOOK & COOK APPROACH

Welcome to **Italian Country Cooking** and the *Look & Cook* series. These volumes are designed to be the simplest, most informative cookbooks you'll ever own. They are the closest I can come to sharing my personal techniques for cooking my favorite recipes without actually being with you in the kitchen.

EQUIPMENT

Equipment and ingredients often determine whether or not you can cook a particular dish, so *Look & Cook* illustrates everything you need at the beginning of each recipe. You'll see at a glance how long a recipe takes to cook, how many servings it makes, what the finished dish looks like, and how much preparation can be done ahead. When you start to cook, you will find that the preparation and cooking are organized into easy-to-follow steps. Each stage has its own color coding, and everything is shown in photographs with brief text accompanying each step. You will never be in doubt as to what it is you are doing, why you are doing it, or how it should look.

INGREDIENTS

🍽 SERVES 4–6   🥄 WORK TIME 25–35 MINUTES   🍲 COOKING TIME 20–30 MINUTES

I've also included helpful hints and ideas under "Anne Says." These may list an alternative ingredient or piece of equipment, or explain the reason for using a certain method, or offer advice on mastering a particular technique. Similarly, if there is a crucial stage in a recipe when things can go wrong, I've included some warnings called "Take Care."

Many of the photographs are annotated to pinpoint why a certain piece of equipment works best, or how food should look at that stage of cooking. Because presentation is so important, there is a picture of the finished dish at the end of each recipe, often with serving suggestions.

Thanks to all this information, you can't go wrong. I'll be with you every step of the way. So please come with me into the kitchen to look, cook, and create some delicious recipes from **Italian Country Cooking**.

WHY ITALIAN COUNTRY COOKING?

The Italians I know look to the countryside for the authentic food of the people. They never think in terms of a national cuisine, but rather in terms of Italy's provinces, each of which has developed its own distinctive cooking style and traditions.

Simplicity is a common theme. The cook uses just a few techniques to feed the family on a daily basis. Kitchens are devoid of gadgets, and standard utensils are kept to a minimum. Until after World War II, even ovens were a luxury in the country kitchen. Roasting was done on the hearth, and bread baking was a once-weekly event in the communal oven. Until very recently, a housewife was taught to cook by her mother and her grandmother, carrying their recipes in her head. If she were lucky, there would be an heirloom notebook of family favorites to serve as an aide mémoire.

Though apparently limited by equipment, technique, and repertoire, the Italian cook is blessed with the greatest gift of all: fine ingredients. Seasonal foods at their peak of flavor form the cornerstone of Italian country cooking. Cooks set out to make the most of what they have, and taste is the prime concern. The humble carrot bursts with flavor when it is simmered until meltingly soft. The much-used method of simmering meats partially covered with liquid ensures they do not dry out during lengthy cooking, while distinct flavors meld in the process. The popular agrodolce, *or sweet-sour, combinations emphasize balance rather than contrast. If the dish turns out to be a visual knockout too, so much the better, but don't expect elaborate presentations and garnishes in the Italian countryside.*

The traditional menu is composed of a succession of modest courses adding up to a substantial

meal. A primo piatto, or first course, of polenta, pasta, or risotto is followed, after a suitable interval, by the secondo piatto *of fish, poultry, or meat, with vegetables or salad. Fruit and/or cheese usually brings the meal to a close. Desserts tend to be reserved for special occasions, such as birthdays and Christmas, as does the* antipasto, *a light dish served before the main meal, or* pasto.

However, the whole style of eating is changing. The main meal always used to be served at mid-day, but modern schedules make such timing impractical, especially in big cities, so that dinner has become more important. At the same time, with the move toward lighter eating, what was once the primo piatto *now often becomes the entire meal.*

What has not changed, and surely never will, is the Italian passion for good food. Nearly everyone you meet in Italy is an authority, quoting a guiding genius who presides over the family kitchen. It is a spirit that can be translated into any language and can flourish anywhere in the world. It is the essence of Italian country cooking – a respect for good ingredients and a desire to make the most of them in the simplest way possible.

RECIPE CHOICE

An Italian cook tries to plan a meal around the produce available in the local market, and I like to do the same. Hearty meals stave off the winter cold and lighter ones welcome a warm spring day. Summer is the time to choose recipes abundant in fresh vegetables and aromatic herbs. Below is a summary of recipes you will find in this volume.

ANTIPASTI AND PRIMI PIATTI

Roman-Style Artichokes with Herbs and Garlic (Carciofi alla Romana): in an unusual presentation, young artichokes are stuffed with parsley, mint, and garlic, then braised and served with their stems pointing upward. *Slow-Braised Artichoke Bottoms (Carciofi in Umido)*: here artichokes are cut into wedges, then cooked with the same herbs, for a different result. *Broiled Mussels with Bell Pepper Topping (Cozze Gratinate)*: salty-tasting mussels are steamed, topped with chopped roasted red bell pepper, parsley, garlic, and breadcrumbs, then broiled. *Broiled Clams (Vongole Gratinate)*: succulent clams are covered with the same savory topping as the mussels. *Broiled Mussels with Parsley and Capers (Cozze al Prezzemolo e Capperi)*: parsley, capers, garlic, and breadcrumbs highlight the delicate flavor of mussels. *Baked Polenta with Wild Mushrooms and Fontina (Polenta Pasticciata)*: meaty wild mushrooms are simmered in white wine and stock, then baked with layers of polenta and fontina cheese. *Baked Polenta with Prosciutto and Eggs (Polenta Pasticciata con Prosciutto e Uova)*: ham and eggs are baked within polenta layers. *Straw and Hay Pasta with Cream, Ham, and Mushrooms (Paglia e Fieno alla Ghiottona)*: homemade white and green fettuccine is embellished with ham, mushrooms, and peas in a rich cream sauce. *Noodles with Sage and Butter (Tonnarelli al Salvia e Burro)*: fresh sage and butter complement plain and spinach noodles. *Shrimp Risotto (Risotto ai Gamberi)*: creamy white rice and pink shrimp make an elegant first course. *Asparagus Risotto (Risotto con gli Asparagi)*: spring is the season to cook asparagus risotto. *Quills with Spicy Tomato and Bacon Sauce (Penne all'Arrabbiata)*: quill-shaped pasta is tossed in a lively tomato sauce with hot red chili pepper, crisp bacon, and mushrooms. *Spaghetti with Tomato and Chili Sauce (Spaghetti alla Satana)*: an even spicier tomato sauce coats spaghetti. *Baked Rigatoni with Meatballs (Timballo di Rigatoni)*: tiny meatballs flavored with Parmesan are hidden between layers of pasta and tomato sauce – hearty enough

for a complete meal. *Baked Ziti with Mozzarella and Olives (Timballo di Ziti con Mozzarella e Olive)*: mozzarella cheese, salty black olives, and tomato sauce flavored with anchovies lend a Mediterranean taste to baked ziti. *Fresh Polenta with Vegetable Stew (Polenta con Fricandò)*: a selection of vegetables is served on a bed of polenta. *Grilled Polenta with Vegetable Stew (Quadrati di Polenta con Fricandò)*: a similar vegetable stew is served with grilled polenta squares. *Spinach and Potato Gnocchi in Tomato-Cream Sauce (Gnocchi Verdi al Sugo di Pomodoro e Panna)*: tomato-cream sauce complements little potato dumplings flavored with spinach. *Spinach and Potato Gnocchi with Cheese (Gnocchi Verdi alla Bava)*: the lightness of potato gnocchi can be fully appreciated in this simple dish served with melted cheese. *Plain Gnocchi with Gorgonzola Sauce (Gnocchi al Gorgonzola)*: blue-veined Gorgonzola, fresh thyme, and cream form the sauce for these plain gnocchi.

SECONDI PIATTI

Sole Fillets Marinated in Vinegar (Sfogi in Saor): in this traditional Venetian dish, strips of sole are pan-fried, then marinated in a sweet-sour mixture of onion, red wine vinegar, and raisins, with pine nuts. *Sole Fillets Marinated with Vinegar and Saffron (Pesce a Scapece)*: saffron lends a golden hue to the sole. *Beef Braised in Red Wine (Stufato di Manzo al Barbera)*: a version of the famed pot roast; beef is browned in olive oil, then cooked in the oven in red wine and beef stock.

Braised Lamb with Potatoes and Tomatoes (Agnello al Forno con Patate e Pomodori): in this classic dish from the South, lamb is braised in the oven with white wine, tomatoes, and potatoes. *Milanese Veal Scaloppine (Scaloppine alla Milanese)*: veal scaloppine at their simple best, coated with Parmesan and breadcrumbs, then sautéed in butter and olive oil, and garnished with lemon slices. *Veal Scaloppine with Prosciutto (Scaloppine alla Modenese)*: a similar preparation adds prosciutto and fontina or Gruyère cheese. *Sautéed Liver and Onions (Fegato alla Veneziana)*: onions are cooked until meltingly soft, then combined with thin slices of sautéed calf's liver in this Venetian classic. *Sautéed Liver with Wine Vinegar (Fegato all'Aceto)*: red wine vinegar and parsley complement quickly sautéed liver. *Deviled Chicken (Pollo alla Diavola)*: a zesty marinade of lemon juice, olive oil, and hot chili pepper flavors and tenderizes chicken before broiling. *Broiled Chicken Drumsticks with Rosemary (Gambe di Pollo ai Ferri)*: easy-to-handle chicken drumsticks are marinated in garlic and rosemary – ideal for a picnic. *Spinach-Stuffed Veal Rolls (Messicani di Vitello)*: veal scaloppine rolled around a stuffing of spinach, Parmesan, and walnuts are served with their cooking liquid. *Roast Pork Loin with Garlic and Rosemary (Arista)*: simple but superb. *Braised Pork with Madeira Sauce (Arrosto di Maiale in Casseruola)*: the pork is braised with onions, and served with carrot batons. *Hunter's Chicken (Pollo alla Cacciatora)*: in this international favorite, chicken is flavored with white wine, garlic, and rosemary, and served with sautéed escarole. *Hunter's Chicken with Black Olives (Pollo alla Cacciatora con le Olive)*: black olives, anchovies, and red wine vinegar add punch to sautéed chicken, while Belgian endive replaces escarole.

DOLCI

Strawberry and Raspberry Hazelnut Tart (Crostata di Fragole e Lamponi): delicate hazelnut pastry, Marsala-flavored whipped cream, and red berries are the perfect conclusion to a special occasion. *Strawberry Tart with Chocolate Cream (Crostata di Fragole al Cioccolato)*: a chocolate lover's dream! *Ricotta Cheesecake (Crostata di Ricotta)*: creamy ricotta cheese forms the background for crunchy almonds, golden raisins, orange zest, and candied orange peel. *Chocolate Ricotta Pie (Crostata di Ricotta al Cioccolato)*: chopped chocolate and orange zest mixed with ricotta fill this rectangular pie – ideal for cutting bite-sized portions. *Walnut Cake with Caramel Topping (Torta di Noci)*: no flour is to be found in this rich, buttery cake. *Walnut Cake with Raisins (Torta di Noci e Uve Passe)*: this is studded with grappa-soaked raisins – the ultimate temptation. *Grapefruit Granita (Granita di Pompelmo)*: frozen grapefruit juice is a refreshing finale to any meal, and can be served with All Souls' Day almond cookies. *Coffee Granita (Granita di Caffè)*: rosettes of Amaretto-flavored whipped cream decorate this frozen dessert. *Apple Cake (Torta di Mele)*: this delicious, moist cake is topped with apple slices, then glazed. *Pear Cake (Torta di Pere)*: caramelized pears replace the apples in this simple variation. *Whipped Cream Cake with Chocolate and Nuts (Zuccotto Toscano)*: sponge cake imbibed with Grand Marnier hides cream, chocolate, and toasted almonds in this domed dessert. *Mocha Whipped Cream Cake (Torta Moka)*: a layered cake filled with mocha-flavored cream and chopped Amaretti cookies.

ITALIAN COUNTRY MENUS

A traditional Italian meal does not depend on a single course, but is made up of at least two principal dishes, and one or two minor ones as well. A vegetable or salad is always served with the *secondo piatto*, while bread is present at every meal. Here are some ideas for three-course menus drawn from the recipes in this book.

For a simple yet elegant dinner, I'd suggest you begin with fragrant Broiled Mussels with Bell Pepper Topping, to be followed by Spinach-Stuffed Veal Rolls. The rolls can be prepared up to 2 days ahead and reheated on the stove, and they make a colorful and attractive presentation when sliced crosswise and arranged on individual plates. For dessert, impress your guests with Ricotta Cheesecake – fresh cheese and almonds, flavored with orange zest, candied orange peel, and golden raisins. What is more, the cheesecake can be completely prepared a day ahead.

Celebrate the approach of summer with a luxurious green Asparagus Risotto. Milanese Veal Scaloppine served with sautéed bell peppers is an equal indulgence, while fresh seasonal berries are combined in Strawberry and Raspberry Hazelnut Tart for a superb finale.

For an autumn dinner, take advantage of seasonal specialties and begin with Baked Polenta with Wild Mushrooms and Fontina, then celebrate the grape harvest with Beef Braised in Red Wine, and bake fresh walnuts in a Walnut Cake with Caramel Topping.

For a simple evening with friends, consider offering Noodles with Sage and Butter followed by Deviled Chicken. Grapefruit or Coffee Granita is a refreshing conclusion, with little All Souls' Day almond cookies.

ROMAN-STYLE ARTICHOKES WITH HERBS AND GARLIC

Carciofi alla Romana

 SERVES 6   WORK TIME 25–30 MINUTES   COOKING TIME 25–45 MINUTES

EQUIPMENT

large heavy-based pan with lid

citrus juicer

slotted spoon

melon baller†

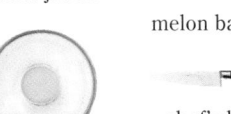

chef's knife

small bowl

small knife

chopping board

†teaspoon can also be used

Young globe artichokes with tender stems are best for this delicious appetizer that can be served warm or at room temperature. The artichokes are hollowed, and filled with chopped parsley, mint, and garlic, then braised to serve with the stems upward. If using older artichokes, you will have to trim away the more fibrous green parts.

GETTING AHEAD

The artichokes can be prepared up to 1 day ahead and refrigerated. Let them come to room temperature before serving.

SHOPPING LIST

6	garlic cloves
1	small bunch of flat-leaf parsley
8–10	sprigs of fresh mint, more for decoration
	salt and pepper
3	lemons
6	young globe artichokes
½ cup	olive oil

INGREDIENTS

garlic cloves

globe artichokes

fresh mint

olive oil

lemons

flat-leaf parsley†

†curly parsley can also be used

ANNE SAYS

"*Look for artichokes of medium size, with tender green leaves. The cut stems should be moist, not dry.*"

ORDER OF WORK

1 PREPARE THE STUFFING AND ARTICHOKES

2 STUFF AND COOK THE ARTICHOKES

1 PREPARE THE STUFFING AND ARTICHOKES

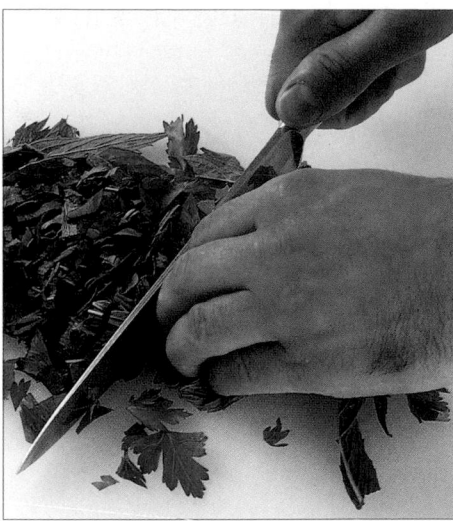

3 Combine the garlic, chopped parsley and mint, and a little salt in the small bowl. Cut 2 lemons in half, and reserve 1 half for adding to the cooking liquid.

1 Set the flat side of the chef's knife on top of each garlic clove and strike it with your fist. Discard the skins and finely chop the garlic.

2 Strip the leaves from the parsley and mint stems. Using the chef's knife, finely chop the leaves.

Cut surfaces of lemon will be used to rub over artichokes and help prevent discoloration

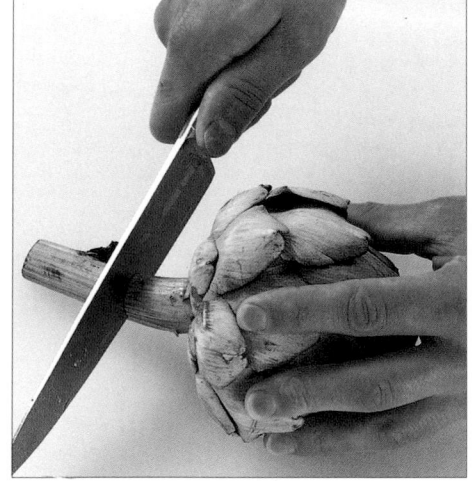

Prickly ends of artichoke leaves can be sharp

5 Snap off the large bottom leaves with your fingers. Continue to remove the leaves, tearing off about three-quarters of each leaf so the edible white part of each one remains attached to the artichoke bottom.

4 Using the chef's knife, trim the tough end of an artichoke stem, leaving about $1^1/_2$ inches of the stem.

Tough fibers are pulled out of artichoke with leaves

6 Continue until you reach the cone of soft, small leaves in the center of the artichoke. Trim the cone of leaves with the chef's knife.

7 Rub the cut edges of the artichoke with a lemon half to prevent discoloration, before continuing with the preparation.

ANNE SAYS
"Coat with lemon at once because the artichoke browns rapidly."

Squeeze lemon as you rub, so juice coats cut surfaces of artichoke

Inner leaves of artichoke are often tinged with purple

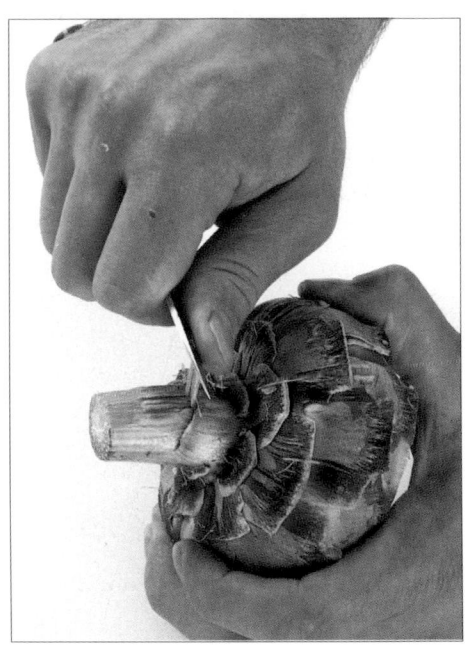

8 With the small knife, peel the stem of the artichoke, cutting away the tough, fibrous exterior.

9 Trim the green parts of the base of the artichoke to remove any of the tough, fibrous leaves.

Melon baller makes light work of removing hairy choke

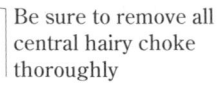

10 Scoop out the choke with the melon baller and squeeze juice from a lemon half into the hollowed-out center of the artichoke. Rub the juice thoroughly around the inside of the artichoke with your finger. Prepare the remaining artichokes in the same way.

Be sure to remove all central hairy choke thoroughly

2 STUFF AND COOK THE ARTICHOKES

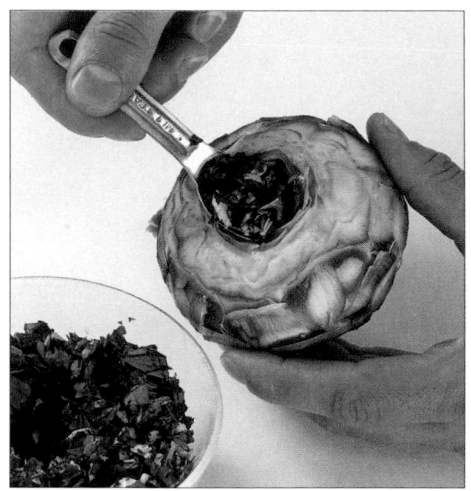

1 Put 2–3 tsp garlic-herb stuffing in the center of an artichoke and press it down well against the bottom and sides. Stuff the remaining artichokes; you should have 2–3 tbsp stuffing left over.

2 Set the artichokes, tops down and stems upward, in the large pan. Sprinkle the remaining stuffing over the outside of the artichokes, and pour the oil over the top.

ANNE SAYS
"The artichokes should just fill the pan in a single layer."

Good quality olive oil adds extra flavor when braising artichokes

3 Sprinkle the artichokes with salt and pepper, and add enough water to come halfway up the sides, not including the stems.

4 Bring to a boil, then cover the pan and simmer the artichokes 25–45 minutes, depending on their age. Add more water to the pan, if necessary, so the artichokes are always half covered.

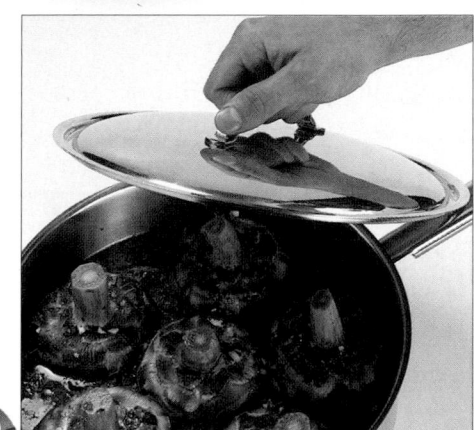

Test for tenderness with tip of knife only

5 To test if the artichokes are cooked, pierce them with the point of the small knife; they should be tender.

Cooking liquid is fragrant with herbs, garlic, and olive oil

6 Using the slotted spoon, transfer the artichokes to a large serving dish, arranging them in a single layer, stems upward. Boil the cooking liquid in the pan until it is reduced to 1 cup.

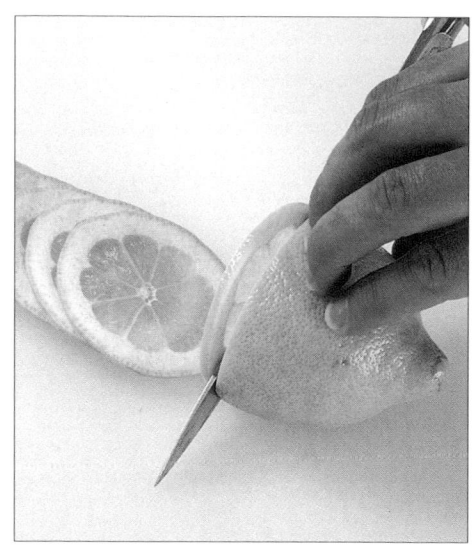

7 With the citrus juicer, squeeze the juice from the reserved lemon half. Remove any seeds from the lemon juice and discard.

8 Add the lemon juice to the cooking liquid and taste for seasoning. Pour over the artichokes and let cool to room temperature.

9 Meanwhile, cut the remaining lemon into slices with the chef's knife, and set them aside until the artichokes are ready to serve.

¶◉¶ TO SERVE

Serve the artichokes at room temperature, decorated with the lemon slices and sprigs of mint.

Lemon juice added to the cooking liquid makes a tangy sauce

Artichokes are served with stems upturned for an unusual presentation

Mint sprigs and lemon slices hint at flavoring of Roman-style artichokes

VARIATION
SLOW-BRAISED ARTICHOKE BOTTOMS

In this recipe, called Carciofi in Umido, *artichoke bottoms are cut into wedges, then braised with the same seasoning as Roman-Style Artichokes for a totally different result.*

Parsley and mint leaves look dainty together

Artichoke wedges are flavored with onion, garlic, and herbs

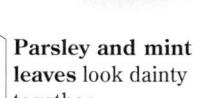

1 Prepare the herbs and garlic as directed in the main recipe, using only 10–12 sprigs of parsley and 3–5 sprigs of mint; do not mix the garlic and chopped herbs together.
2 Peel 1 small onion, leaving a little of the root attached, and cut it lengthwise in half. Lay each onion half flat on the chopping board and slice horizontally toward the root, leaving the slices attached at the root end, and then slice vertically, again leaving the root end uncut. Finally, cut across the onion to make dice.
3 Prepare the artichoke bottoms: remove the stems by snapping them off so that the fibers are pulled out along with the stems.
4 Tear off the leaves as directed, then cut off all the soft cone of leaves and remove the choke.
5 Cut each artichoke bottom into 8 wedges.

6 Squeeze the juice from 1 lemon into a bowl of water and add the empty lemon halves. Put the artichoke wedges in the acidulated water.
7 Heat ¼ cup olive oil in a heavy pan, add the onion and garlic, and cook, stirring, until soft but not brown, 3–5 minutes.
8 Stir in drained artichoke wedges, parsley, mint, salt, and pepper. Add water to half cover the artichoke wedges and bring to a boil.
9 Press a circle of parchment paper on top of the artichokes. Cover the pan and simmer, stirring occasionally, until the artichokes are tender when pierced with a knife, 25–40 minutes, depending on their age. Add more water if necessary, so the artichokes are always half covered.
10 Remove the lid and paper, and bring the cooking liquid to a boil; if necessary, boil until reduced to about ½ cup. Taste for seasoning and set aside to cool.
11 Serve the artichokes warm or at room temperature in individual bowls. Spoon the cooking liquid over the artichokes and decorate with sprigs of parsley and mint.

BROILED MUSSELS WITH BELL PEPPER TOPPING

Cozze Gratinate

 SERVES 4   WORK TIME 25–30 MINUTES   BROILING TIME 1–2 MINUTES

EQUIPMENT

plastic bag

small brush

food processor †

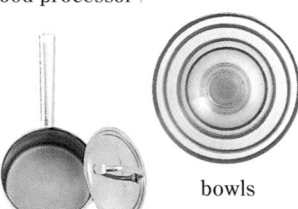

bowls

large saucepan with lid

small knife

rubber spatula

large baking dish

tongs

slotted spoon

chef's knife

paper towels

chopping board

† blender can also be used

True antipasto! This light dish, to be served before the main meal, is perfect for special occasions. The sea-salt flavor of mussels is highlighted by a piquant topping of flat-leaf parsley, garlic, breadcrumbs, and roasted red bell pepper. This is so delicious that you'll want to make it everyday fare.

GETTING AHEAD

The mussels can be cooked and stuffed up to 4 hours ahead. Keep them, tightly covered, in the refrigerator. Broil them just before serving.

SHOPPING LIST

1	small bunch of flat-leaf parsley
1	large red bell pepper
2	garlic cloves
2	slices of white bread
2 tbsp	olive oil
	salt and pepper
24	large mussels, total weight about 1½ lb
1 cup	dry white wine
1	lemon for serving

INGREDIENTS

mussels

flat-leaf parsley †

dry white wine

white bread

olive oil

red bell pepper

garlic cloves

lemon

† curly parsley can also be used

ANNE SAYS
"You may want to buy a few extra mussels to allow for some damaged shells."

ORDER OF WORK

1 MAKE THE TOPPING

2 PREPARE AND COOK THE MUSSELS

3 STUFF AND BROIL THE MUSSELS

1 MAKE THE TOPPING

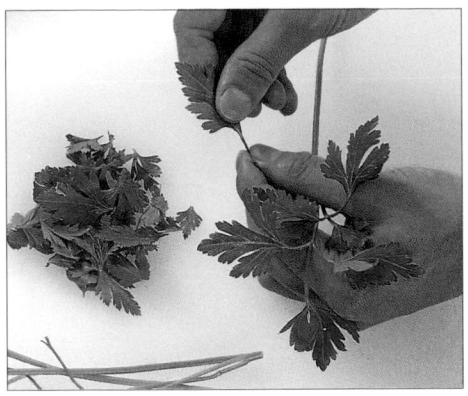

1 Reserving a few sprigs for decoration, strip the parsley leaves from the stems, keeping both the leaves and stems separate.

Pepper is sliced so it is easy to work in processor

Use curved fingers to guide knife blade

2 Roast the red bell pepper (see box, page 18). Cut each bell pepper half lengthwise into strips.

ANNE SAYS
"The bell pepper strips will be worked in the food processor, so it is not necessary to cut them neatly."

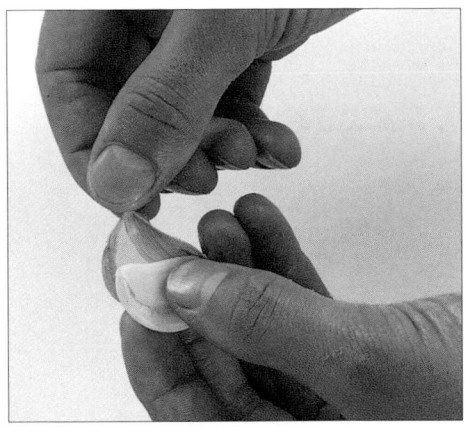

3 To peel the garlic, set the flat side of the chef's knife on each clove and strike it. Discard the skins.

4 Using the chef's knife, trim and discard the crusts from the bread slices. Cut the bread into cubes.

ITALIAN HERBS

A visit to any Italian vegetable market demonstrates the country's abundance of fresh herbs. Oregano, basil, and flat-leaf parsley, in particular, are used widely in Italian cooking.

Oregano, *which is actually a wild variety of marjoram, is native to the Mediterranean region. It has a more pronounced flavor than marjoram, and appears in many Italian dishes, especially tomato sauces, stews, and pizza. It can be used fresh or dried.*

Basil *is one of the most important herbs in Italian cooking. It complements many flavors, but has a special affinity with tomatoes – a favorite Italian salad is fresh basil leaves scattered over sliced tomatoes drizzled with fruity extra-virgin olive oil. It is best to use fresh basil when specified in recipes because dried basil does not have the same flavor – it tastes more minty. Italian cooks preserve their basil crops by filling jars with the leaves, lightly salting them, then topping up with olive oil.*

Flat-Leaf Parsley *is native to southern Europe, and widely used in Italian cooking. Flat-leaf parsley is preferred by Italian cooks to curly parsley, because it has a deeper, more pungent flavor, and because it stands up far better to heat in cooked dishes. However, both types are interchangeable in recipes, so if you find curly parsley easier to obtain, it can be substituted wherever flat-leaf parsley is specified.*

5 Work the cubes of bread in the food processor to form crumbs. Add the parsley leaves, peeled garlic cloves, olive oil, and the roasted red pepper strips to the food processor.

Food processor makes it quick and easy to chop ingredients for topping

Flat-leaf parsley has robust flavor

6 Work the ingredients to a purée. Season the mixture to taste with salt and pepper. Alternatively, chop the parsley leaves, garlic, and roasted red pepper by hand with the chef's knife, then stir in the breadcrumbs and oil; you will have a coarser topping.

HOW TO ROAST, PEEL, AND SEED BELL PEPPERS

Roasting bell peppers under the broiler makes them easy to peel and gives them a smoky flavor. After they are roasted, peeled, and cored, peppers can be stuffed whole, sliced and added to salads, or cooked alone or with other vegetables.

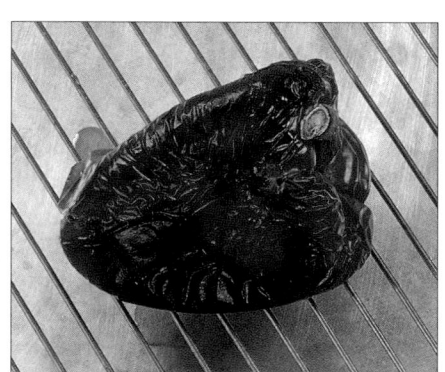

1 Heat the broiler. Set the whole pepper on a rack about 4 inches from the heat. Broil the pepper, turning as needed, until the skin is black and blistered all over, 10–12 minutes.

2 Seal the pepper in a plastic bag and let cool so the skin is loosened by the steam trapped inside.

Roasted bell peppers are tender and full of flavor

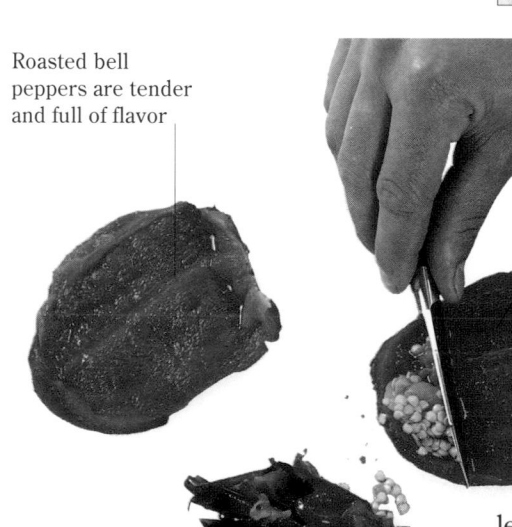

Flatten pepper half so seeds are easy to scrape off

3 With a small knife, peel off the skin. Rinse the pepper under running water and pat dry with paper towels.

4 Cut out the core, then slit pepper lengthwise in half. Scrape out seeds and white ribs with the knife blade.

2 PREPARE AND COOK THE MUSSELS

1 Clean the mussels: scrape them with the small knife to remove any barnacles.

Back of knife is used for scraping off barnacles

Shells are cleaned to make attractive presentation

2 Using the small knife, detach and discard any weeds or "beards" from the mussels.

3 Scrub the mussels under cold running water with the small brush.

4 Discard any mussels that have broken shells or that do not close when tapped.

! TAKE CARE !
Only cook mussels that are in good condition.

5 Put the wine and parsley stems in the saucepan. Bring to a boil and simmer 2 minutes. Add the mussels.

6 Cover and cook over high heat, stirring once, until the mussels open, 2–3 minutes. Transfer them to a large bowl with the slotted spoon. Discard any mussels that have not opened at this point.

Stir mussels once during cooking so they steam evenly

Parsley stems add flavor to cooking liquid

ANNE SAYS
"If you like, strain the flavorful cooking liquid from mussels to use as fish stock."

3 STUFF AND BROIL THE MUSSELS

1 Heat the broiler. Remove the top shell from each mussel and discard the rubbery ring surrounding the meat.

2 Using a teaspoon, spoon a little of the roasted bell pepper topping onto each of the mussels.

Red bell pepper topping conceals mussels underneath

Mussels should fit snugly into baking dish

3 Set the mussels in their bottom shells in the baking dish. Broil until very hot and the topping is heated through, 1–2 minutes. Cut the lemon into wedges and set aside for serving.

🍴 **TO SERVE**
Arrange the mussels, fanned in circles, on warmed individual plates, with a lemon wedge on the side of each. Decorate with a parsley sprig.

Lemon juice is delicious on piping hot mussels

Red pepper topping makes colorful contrast to black mussel shells

BROILED CLAMS

Cherrystone clams are featured here in Vongole Gratinate *although steamers are a delicious alternative.*

1 Make the roasted bell pepper topping as directed in the main recipe.
2 Substitute 36 small or 24 medium undamaged, live clams for the mussels and scrub them; unlike mussels, clams do not have barnacles or weeds.

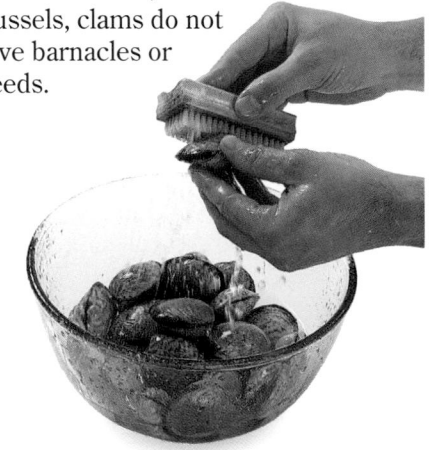

3 Cook the clams as directed in the main recipe, allowing 3–5 minutes for the clams to open, or longer if the shells are very thick.
4 Meanwhile, thinly slice a lemon for decoration. Cut each lemon slice from center to edge, and twist each edge in opposite directions.
5 Discard the black skin covering the neck of each clam, nipping it off with your fingers. Spoon the topping over the clams and broil them as directed.
6 Serve them on warmed individual plates. Decorate each plate with a lemon twist and parsley sprigs.

BROILED MUSSELS WITH PARSLEY AND CAPERS

Capers replace the roasted red bell pepper in Cozze al Prezzemolo e Capperi.

Lemon slices are refreshing decoration

Caper topping is piquant complement to mussels

1 Omit the red bell pepper from the main recipe. Peel 4 garlic cloves and drain 1 tbsp capers in a small strainer.
2 Make the topping as directed, adding 2 tbsp freshly grated Parmesan cheese to the breadcrumbs with the garlic, parsley, and oil, and replacing the bell pepper with the capers. Taste for seasoning.

Capers add piquancy

3 Steam the mussels and remove the top shells as directed. Spoon the topping over the mussels.

4 Arrange the mussels in gratin dishes and sprinkle with 2 tbsp freshly grated Parmesan cheese; broil as directed. Decorate with half slices of lemon.

BAKED POLENTA WITH WILD MUSHROOMS AND FONTINA

Polenta Pasticciata

 SERVES 6   WORK TIME 40–45 MINUTES* BAKING TIME 20–25 MINUTES

EQUIPMENT

large saucepan

medium frying pan

paper towels

metal spatula

2 baking sheets

bowls

wooden spoon

small knife

whisk

chef's knife

pastry brush

9- x 13-inch baking dish

chopping board

Polenta was once daily fare in parts of Italy, so there are many tempting recipes for it. Here it is sliced and baked with wild mushrooms and cheese.

GETTING AHEAD

The dish can be prepared up to 1 day ahead and refrigerated. Bake as directed in the recipe.

*plus 1 hour chilling time

INGREDIENTS

fresh chanterelles

common mushrooms

fresh thyme

fontina cheese†

yellow cornmeal

olive oil

dry white wine

heavy cream

garlic cloves

beef stock

† mozzarella, Gouda, or Edam can also be used

ANNE SAYS
"If using dried mushrooms, soak in 1 cup warm water until plump, 30 minutes. Drain, and reserve liquid."

ORDER OF WORK

1 MAKE THE POLENTA

2 MAKE THE MUSHROOM STEW

3 BAKE THE PASTICCIATA

SHOPPING LIST

1½ quarts	water
1 tbsp	salt
2½ cups	yellow cornmeal
	For the wild mushroom stew
½ lb	fresh wild mushrooms, such as chanterelles or boletus, or 2 oz dried wild mushrooms
¾ lb	common mushrooms
3	garlic cloves
5–7	sprigs of fresh thyme or rosemary
3 tbsp	olive oil, more for baking dish
½ cup	dry white wine
1 cup	beef stock (see box, page 122) or water
¼ cup	heavy cream
	salt and pepper
½ lb	fontina cheese

1 MAKE THE POLENTA

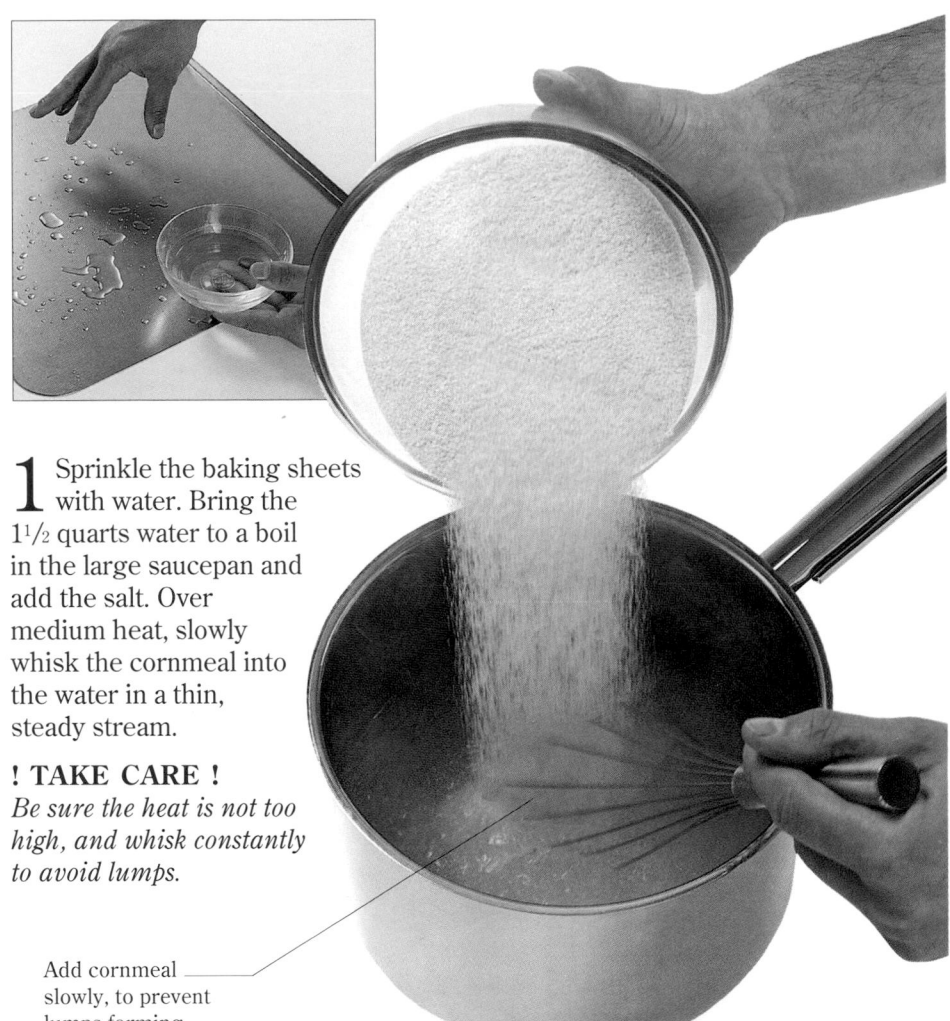

1 Sprinkle the baking sheets with water. Bring the 1½ quarts water to a boil in the large saucepan and add the salt. Over medium heat, slowly whisk the cornmeal into the water in a thin, steady stream.

! TAKE CARE !
Be sure the heat is not too high, and whisk constantly to avoid lumps.

Add cornmeal slowly, to prevent lumps forming

2 Cook the mixture, stirring to prevent sticking, until thick enough to pull away from the side of the pan, 10–15 minutes. The polenta mixture should be soft and smooth.

3 Spread the polenta evenly on the moistened baking sheets, in a layer about 12 inches square and ⅜-inch thick on each sheet. Let cool, then chill until very firm, 1 hour.

2 MAKE THE MUSHROOM STEW

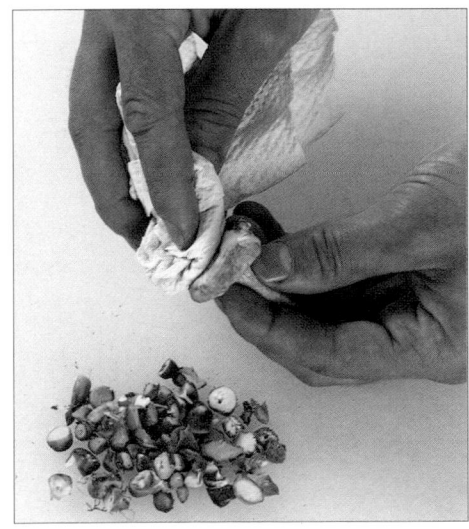

1 Wipe the fresh wild mushrooms and common mushrooms with damp paper towels, and trim the stems.

Wild mushrooms have delicious flavor

2 Cut the wild mushrooms into slices and the common mushrooms into quarters. Small wild mushrooms need only be cut in half.

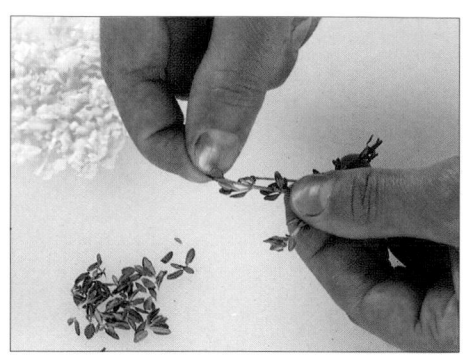

3 Set the flat side of the chef's knife on top of each garlic clove and strike it with your fist. Discard the skins and finely chop the garlic. Strip the thyme leaves from the stems.

4 Heat the olive oil in the frying pan. Add the mushrooms, garlic, and thyme and cook, stirring, until the mushrooms are tender and all the liquid has evaporated, 5–7 minutes.

Heavy cream binds mushroom stew

Mushroom mixture is rich and juicy

5 Add the wine and simmer until almost evaporated, 2–3 minutes. Add the stock or water if using fresh wild mushrooms (or the soaking liquid if using dried mushrooms) and continue cooking until reduced by half, 5–7 minutes. Stir in the cream until the liquid thickens slightly, 1–2 minutes. Season to taste with salt and pepper.

3 BAKE THE PASTICCIATA

1 Heat the oven to 425° F. Brush the baking dish with olive oil. Cut the rind from the fontina cheese and cut the cheese into thin even slices.

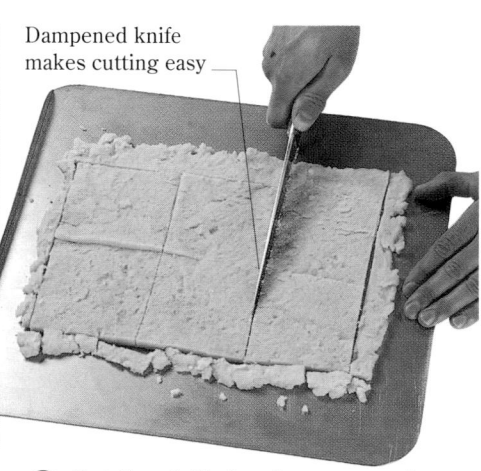

Dampened knife makes cutting easy

2 Cut the chilled polenta on each baking sheet into 6 even-sized pieces. Trim them into 4-inch squares so they will fit evenly in the baking dish; reserve the trimmings.

3 Arrange half of the polenta squares in the bottom of the prepared baking dish, placing them side by side in a single layer.

4 Spoon half of the mushroom stew over the polenta, spreading the mushrooms evenly over the squares.

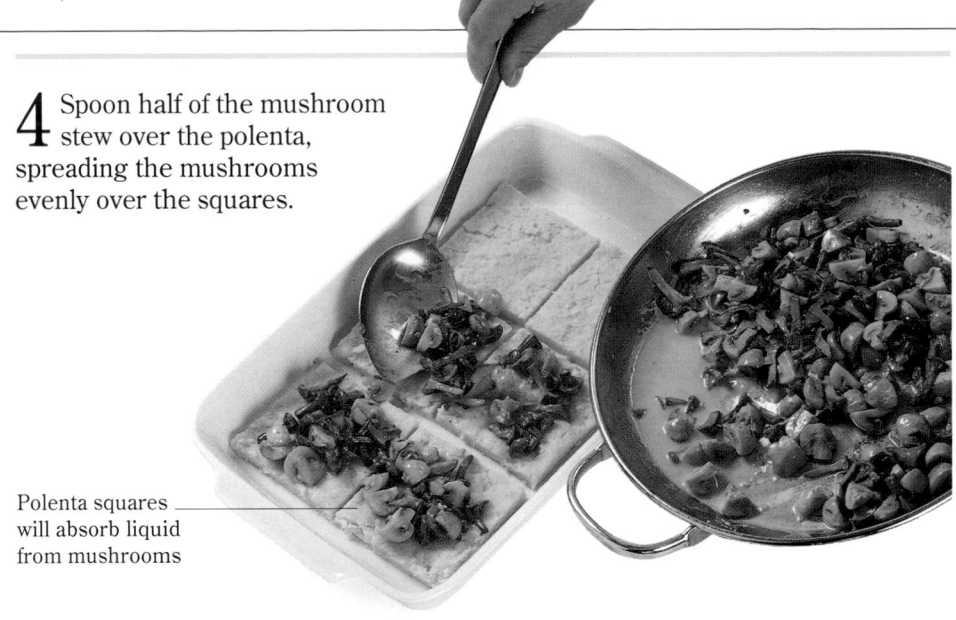

Polenta squares will absorb liquid from mushrooms

Fontina cheese melts into mushroom mixture

5 Arrange half of the sliced fontina on top. Repeat with another layer of the remaining polenta and mushrooms. Cut the polenta trimmings into small squares and arrange them over the mushrooms. Top with the remaining fontina slices. Bake the pasticciata in the heated oven until the cheese is melted and the polenta and mushrooms are very hot, 20–25 minutes.

¶◎¶ TO SERVE
Transfer squares of pasticciata directly from the baking dish onto warmed plates.

VARIATION

BAKED POLENTA WITH PROSCIUTTO AND EGGS

In Polenta Pasticciata con Prosciutto e Uova, *polenta is baked with diced prosciutto, beaten egg, and grated Parmesan.*

1 Make the polenta as directed in the main recipe, using 2 cups cornmeal and 1¼ quarts water. Spread the cooked polenta on 2 moistened baking sheets, as directed, and let cool; chill until firm. Cut the polenta into twelve 4-inch squares.

2 Omit the wild mushroom stew and fontina cheese. Chop 4 oz thinly sliced prosciutto. Beat 2 eggs and season them with pepper.

3 Brush an 8-inch square dish with olive oil. Arrange one-third of the polenta squares in the dish and spoon over half of the beaten egg. Sprinkle with half of the chopped prosciutto and ¼ cup freshly grated Parmesan cheese.

4 Top with half of the remaining polenta, the remaining egg and prosciutto, and ¼ cup freshly grated Parmesan. Arrange the remaining polenta squares on top and sprinkle with another ¼ cup freshly grated Parmesan cheese.

5 Bake as directed, until the top is golden brown. Serves 4.

Wild mushroom stew and mild fontina cheese make a delicious combination of flavors

STRAW AND HAY PASTA WITH CREAM, HAM, AND MUSHROOMS

Paglia e Fieno alla Ghiottona

 SERVES 6   WORK TIME 55–60 MINUTES* COOKING TIME 2–4 MINUTES

EQUIPMENT

pasta machine

wooden spoon

chef's knife

large frying pan

large forks

colander

metal spatula

paper towels

large pot

bowls

chopping board

INGREDIENTS

cooked ham

Parmesan cheese

flour

eggs

ground nutmeg

frozen spinach

onion

fresh green peas

heavy cream

mushrooms

butter

This dish of green and white fettuccine (representing straw and hay), ham, mushrooms, and peas in a cream sauce would appeal to any gourmand, or ghiottone *in Italian.*

plus 3–4 hours standing time

SHOPPING LIST

1/2 lb	mushrooms
4 oz	sliced cooked ham
1	small onion
1/4 cup	butter
3/4 cup	shelled fresh green peas or defrosted peas
1 cup	heavy cream
1	pinch of ground nutmeg
1/2 cup	freshly grated Parmesan cheese for serving
	salt and pepper
	For the plain fettuccine
1 1/2 cups	flour, more if needed
2	eggs
	For the spinach fettuccine
2 tbsp	defrosted spinach
1 3/4 cups	flour, more if needed
2	eggs

ORDER OF WORK

1 MAKE THE PLAIN AND SPINACH PASTA DOUGH

2 KNEAD, ROLL, AND CUT THE PASTA

3 PREPARE SAUCE

4 COOK THE PASTA

1 MAKE THE PLAIN AND SPINACH PASTA DOUGH

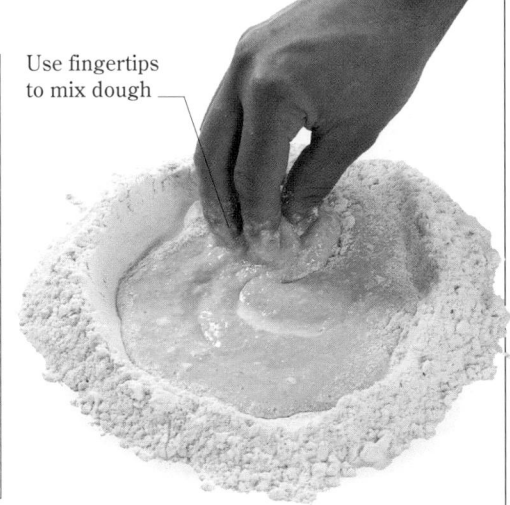

Use fingertips to mix dough

1 Make the plain pasta dough: sift the flour onto the work surface in a mound, using a strainer or a flour sifter. With your fingers, make a well in the center of the flour.

2 Lightly beat the eggs with a fork and add, with ½ tsp salt, to the well in the flour.

3 Gradually mix in the flour from the sides to make a firm dough. If the dough is sticky, add more flour.

Use heel of your hand to knead dough

4 As you mix, use the metal spatula to scrape up bits of dough that stick to the work surface.

ANNE SAYS
"The dough may appear dry and floury at first, but will become more moist as the flour absorbs the eggs."

5 On a floured work surface, press the dough together into a ball. Knead it with the heel of your hand to blend. Cover the dough with a bowl and leave to rest, 1 hour. Meanwhile, make the spinach pasta dough.

ANNE SAYS
"If you are short of time or do not have a pasta machine, you can substitute 10 oz fresh or dried store-bought noodles, cooking them 1–2 minutes for fresh, 7–10 minutes for dried, or according to package directions."

6 For the spinach pasta dough: squeeze the defrosted spinach in your fist to remove all excess water. Finely chop it with the chef's knife.

7 Make the pasta dough as for the plain dough, adding the spinach with the eggs and salt. Leave the dough to rest, covered with a bowl, 1 hour.

Spinach dough is green, representing hay

Plain pasta dough is light gold like straw

2 KNEAD, ROLL, AND CUT THE PASTA

1 Using the metal spatula, cut the ball of spinach dough into 3 or 4 pieces of more or less equal size. Set the pasta machine rollers on their widest setting.

2 Flour 1 piece of spinach dough lightly and feed it through the rollers of the machine.

3 Fold the dough strip into thirds or quarters to make a square, then feed it through the machine rollers again, dusting with flour if the dough sticks. Repeat this folding and rolling process 7–10 times to knead the dough until it is smooth and elastic.

4 Tighten the pasta machine rollers 1 notch and feed the dough through them.

5 Continue rolling the pasta dough, tightening the rollers 1 notch each time, ending with the rollers on their narrowest setting.

Catch dough as it comes through rollers

6 Lightly dust the dough with flour, if necessary, so that it does not stick to the rollers. When the dough is ready, it will be satiny smooth and will no longer crack at the sides as it comes out of the rollers.

Handle thin dough carefully

Broom handle is ideal for drying pasta

7 Hang the sheet of pasta over a clean broom handle, or over the edge of the work surface, and let dry until the pasta has a leathery look, 5–10 minutes. Meanwhile, knead and roll out the remaining pieces of spinach dough and hang them over the broom handle.

8 With the chef's knife or scissors, cut the sheets of dough into lengths of about 12 inches.

Hang up pasta dough to dry

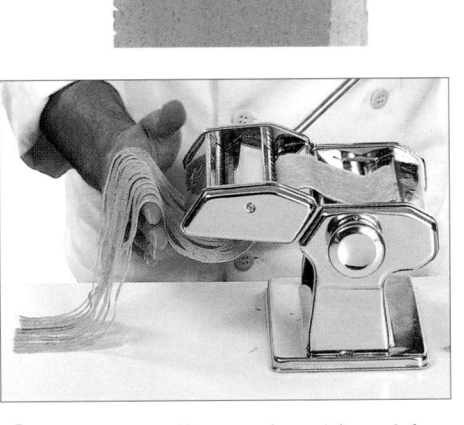

9 Fit the handle into the wider of the machine's cutters and feed 1 sheet of dough through the machine. As the fettuccine strips emerge, catch them on your hand.

10 Toss the fettuccine with a little flour, then coil loosely into a bundle around your fingers. Repeat with the remaining sheets of spinach dough, then repeat the process for the plain pasta dough. Let dry, 1–2 hours.

3 PREPARE SAUCE

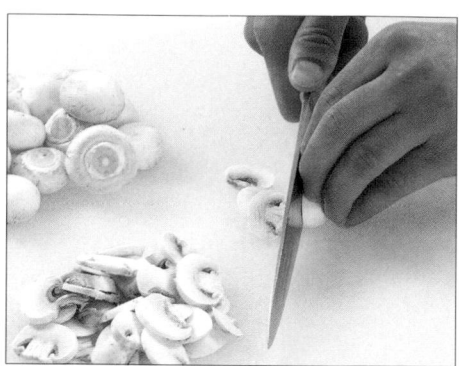

1 Wipe the mushroom caps with damp paper towels and trim the stems even with the caps. Set the mushrooms stem-side down and slice them.

2 Cut the ham into thin strips. Peel the onion and cut it lengthwise in half. Lay each half flat and slice it horizontally and then vertically. Finally, cut into fine dice.

Heavy cream thickens sauce

3 Heat half of the butter in the large frying pan. Add the onion and cook, stirring occasionally with the wooden spoon, until soft, 3–5 minutes. Add the sliced mushrooms with salt and pepper and continue cooking until the liquid evaporates, 5–7 minutes.

4 Add the ham strips, peas, and heavy cream to the onions and mushrooms. Stir and heat to boiling, then simmer until slightly reduced, 1–2 minutes. Add the ground nutmeg to the sauce and taste for seasoning.

4 COOK THE PASTA

1 Fill the large pot with water, bring to a boil, and add 1 tbsp salt. Add the plain and spinach fettuccine and simmer until just tender but still chewy, 1–2 minutes, stirring occasionally to prevent sticking.

ANNE SAYS
"Test by tasting the pasta – it should be chewy, or al dente."

Water loses heat momentarily when pasta is added

2 Drain the fettuccine thoroughly in the colander, rinse with hot water to wash away the starch, and drain again thoroughly.

Toss pasta in butter before adding sauce

3 Melt the remaining butter in the pot and add the fettuccine. Toss with the butter over medium heat, then add the sauce, and continue tossing until coated and very hot, 1–2 minutes. Take from the heat, sprinkle generously with some of the freshly grated Parmesan cheese, and toss again.

Parmesan cheese is sprinkled on top of each serving as a finishing touch

¶⊙¶ TO SERVE
Pile the pasta in warmed individual bowls and serve with the remaining Parmesan cheese.

Ham is outstanding ingredient in cream sauce

VARIATION

NOODLES WITH SAGE AND BUTTER

In this version of straw and hay pasta, Tonnarelli al Salvia e Burro, *skinny noodles replace the fettuccine, with a simple topping of chopped fresh sage and melted butter.*

1 Make, knead, and roll the plain and spinach pasta dough as directed, ending with the rollers at the third narrowest setting; the dough should be about ⅛-inch thick.
2 Cut the dough into 6-inch lengths, then cut them with the pasta machine, using the narrower of the machine's cutters – they should be the shape of squared spaghetti. Dry the noodles as directed in the main recipe.
3 Omit the cream sauce. Strip the leaves from 1 medium bunch of fresh sage and pile them on a chopping board. With a chef's knife, coarsely chop the leaves.
4 Cook and drain the pasta and put it in a warmed serving bowl. Add ½ cup butter cut into small pieces, and sprinkle the chopped sage on the top.
5 Toss until all the strands of pasta are coated with melted butter and chopped sage. Season with salt and pepper. Serve freshly grated Parmesan cheese separately.

GETTING AHEAD

The noodles can be made, dried, and stored, loosely wrapped, in the refrigerator up to 48 hours, or they can be frozen. Sprinkle them lightly with flour so that the pieces do not stick together. Prepare the sauce and cook the pasta just before serving.

SHRIMP RISOTTO

Risotto ai Gamberi

 SERVES 6   WORK TIME 15–20 MINUTES   COOKING TIME 25–30 MINUTES*

EQUIPMENT

chef's knife

small knife   small bowl

saucepans

wooden spoon

ladle

slotted spoon

chopping board

The best risotto is made with short-grain Italian Arborio rice, simmered until al dente – smooth and creamy but slightly firm to the bite. Stock is added gradually and you must stir constantly – tedious, but the results are well worth it. Once the risotto is made, do not leave it to stand or it will become heavy.

— GETTING AHEAD —

Freshly made risotto is incomparable; there is really no satisfactory way to reheat it or keep it warm.

*At no time during the cooking of the risotto can you leave the kitchen, as the risotto must be stirred constantly. This is most important to remember when calculating your total work time.

INGREDIENTS

raw shrimp

Arborio rice†

fish stock

garlic cloves

flat-leaf parsley‡

dry white wine

olive oil

onion

† other short-grain or medium-grain rice can also be used
‡ curly parsley can also be used

ANNE SAYS
"Do not worry if you are short on stock. You can use more water instead, adding just a small amount of stock to flavor the risotto."

ANNE SAYS
"Make sure that the saucepan you use for cooking the rice is large enough to allow room for expansion. A heavy-based saucepan is essential, to prevent the rice sticking to the bottom."

SHOPPING LIST

1 lb	small or medium raw shrimp
2	garlic cloves
1	small bunch of flat-leaf parsley
6 tbsp	olive oil
	salt and pepper
¼ cup	dry white wine
1 quart	fish stock or mild chicken stock (see boxes, page 123)
1 cup	water, more if needed
1	medium onion
2 cups	Arborio rice

ORDER OF WORK

1 PREPARE THE SHRIMP AND COOKING LIQUID

2 COOK THE RICE AND ADD THE SHRIMP

1 PREPARE THE SHRIMP AND COOKING LIQUID

Shrimp shells come off easily in your fingers

1 Peel off the shrimp shells with your fingers. Make a shallow cut along the back of each peeled shrimp with the small knife and remove the dark intestinal vein.

2 Set the flat side of the chef's knife on top of each garlic clove and strike it with your fist. Peel and finely chop the garlic. Strip the parsley leaves from the stems, reserving 6 sprigs for garnish. Pile the leaves on the chopping board and coarsely chop them.

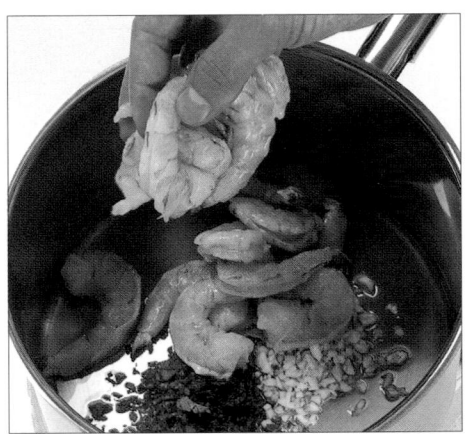

3 Heat one-third of the oil in a medium saucepan and add the garlic, parsley, peeled shrimp, salt, and pepper.

Pink shrimp are perfumed with garlic, parsley, and white wine

4 Cook, stirring with the slotted spoon, just until the shrimp turn pink, 1–2 minutes. Pour in the wine and stir thoroughly.

5 Transfer the shrimp to the bowl; set aside. Simmer the liquid in the pan until reduced by three-quarters, 2–3 minutes. Add the stock and 1 cup water to the cooking liquid and heat to boiling. Keep the liquid simmering.

2 COOK THE RICE AND ADD THE SHRIMP

1 Peel the onion, leaving a little of the root attached, and cut lengthwise in half. Slice each half horizontally toward the root, leaving the slices attached at the root end. Then slice vertically, again leaving the root end uncut. Cut across the onion to make dice.

2 Heat half of the remaining oil in a large saucepan. Add the onion and cook, stirring with the wooden spoon, until soft but not brown, 2–3 minutes.

3 Add the rice to the pan and stir until shiny and coated with oil. Using the ladle, pour in just enough of the simmering liquid to cover the rice.

Rice will start absorbing liquid quickly

Liquid for risotto can be fish stock or chicken stock

4 Simmer the rice, stirring constantly until all the liquid is absorbed, 3–5 minutes. Add more liquid just to cover the rice and simmer, stirring, until completely absorbed.

5 Continue adding liquid to the rice in this way. Stir constantly, and make sure all the liquid is absorbed before adding more.

Creamy rice will take on flavor from shrimp

6 Test the rice from time to time toward the end of the cooking. Stop adding liquid when the rice is *al dente* – just tender but firm to the bite. The total cooking time should be 25–30 minutes, and you will need 1–1¼ quarts liquid altogether, adding more water if necessary. Stir in the shrimp and the remaining olive oil, and season with salt and pepper to taste.

ANNE SAYS
"As soon as the rice is tender, stop adding liquid, because you do not want the final result to be too soupy."

TO SERVE
Spoon the risotto into warmed bowls, garnish with the reserved parsley sprigs, and serve immediately.

Perfectly cooked risotto is creamily bound together, neither stiff nor soupy

Fresh shrimp add luxurious touch to traditional risotto

VARIATION

ASPARAGUS RISOTTO

Tender green asparagus sautéed in butter is the basis for Risotto con gli Asparagi.

1 Omit the garlic, parsley, shrimp, white wine, and onion. Peel 2 shallots, if necessary separating the shallots into sections and peeling the sections. On a chopping board, finely dice the shallots.
2 Peel the tough outer skin from 1 lb asparagus and trim off woody ends. Cut the asparagus into ½-inch lengths; set aside the tips.
3 Heat 1¼ quarts mild chicken stock in a saucepan to simmering. Heat about 3 tbsp olive oil in a second saucepan, add the shallots and cook, stirring until soft but not brown, 1–2 minutes.
4 Add the asparagus stems to the shallots, cover the pan, and sauté until they are tender, 2–3 minutes.
5 Stir in the rice as directed. Cook, adding the simmering stock as directed.
6 Add the reserved asparagus tips with the second-to-last batch of liquid; cook about 10 minutes. If you like, some asparagus tips can be cooked separately to use as a garnish. Add to boiling salted water and cook until tender, 2–3 minutes. Drain the asparagus tips and set aside.
7 When the rice is tender, stir in 2 tbsp butter and taste for seasoning. Serve at once in warmed individual bowls, topped with freshly grated Parmesan cheese. Garnish with asparagus tips, if you like.

QUILLS WITH SPICY TOMATO AND BACON SAUCE

Penne all'Arrabbiata

🍽 SERVES 6   🥣 WORK TIME 35–40 MINUTES   🍲 COOKING TIME 30–40 MINUTES

EQUIPMENT

chef's knife

small knife

large pot

bowls

paper towels

large frying pan with lid

wooden spoon

colander

slotted spoon

saucepan

chopping board

rubber gloves

On the whole, Italians do not savor spicy foods, but this is an exception. Here, it is chili pepper that brings a dose of fire to the spicy tomato sauce. With bacon and mushrooms, it coats the pasta, traditionally served as a first course.

GETTING AHEAD
The tomato and bacon sauce can be made up to 2 days ahead and refrigerated. Reheat it on top of the stove and cook the pasta just before serving.

SHOPPING LIST

1 lb	quills
2 tbsp	butter
½ cup	freshly grated Parmesan cheese
	For the spicy tomato and bacon sauce
3 lb	plum or medium tomatoes
1	fresh hot red chili pepper
2	garlic cloves
¾ lb	mushrooms
5–7	sprigs of fresh oregano
4 oz	thick-cut bacon slices
	salt and pepper

INGREDIENTS

quills   plum tomatoes

Parmesan cheese†

fresh oregano   thick-cut bacon slices

mushrooms   butter

fresh hot chili pepper ‡

garlic cloves

† Romano cheese can also be used
‡ dried hot chili pepper can also be used

ANNE SAYS
"*Out of season, I often substitute canned whole plum tomatoes for fresh ones, reserving their juice.*"

ORDER OF WORK

1 MAKE THE SPICY TOMATO AND BACON SAUCE

2 COOK THE QUILLS; FINISH THE DISH

1 MAKE THE SPICY TOMATO AND BACON SAUCE

1 Remove the cores from the tomatoes and score an "x" on the base of each. Immerse in a pan of boiling water until the skins start to split, 8–15 seconds, depending on their ripeness. Transfer to cold water. When cold, peel off the skins, cut the tomatoes crosswise in half, squeeze out the seeds, then coarsely chop each half.

Plum tomatoes are ideal when available

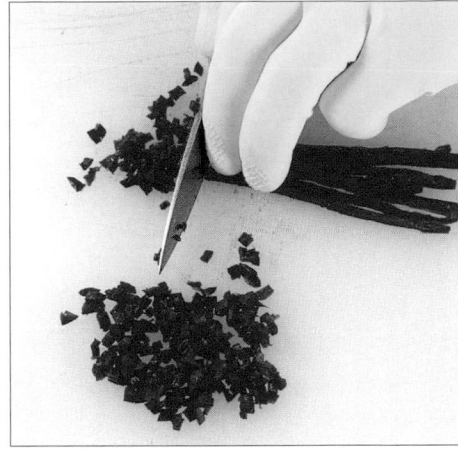

2 Wearing rubber gloves, cut the fresh chili pepper lengthwise in half with the small knife. Cut out the core and fleshy white ribs; scrape out the seeds. Cut each half into very thin strips, hold the strips together, and cut across to make fine dice. If using a dried chili pepper, chop it and discard the seeds.

3 Set the flat side of the chef's knife on top of each garlic clove and strike it with your fist. Discard the skins and finely chop the garlic.

Whole oregano leaves make attractive garnish

4 Wipe the mushrooms with damp paper towels; trim the stems even with the caps. Set the mushrooms stem-side down and slice them.

ANNE SAYS
"I often buy a selection of different mushrooms for added flavor."

5 Strip the oregano leaves from the stems, reserving a few leaves for garnish. Pile the leaves on the chopping board and finely chop them.

6 Stack the slices of bacon on the chopping board and cut across into wide strips, using the chef's knife.

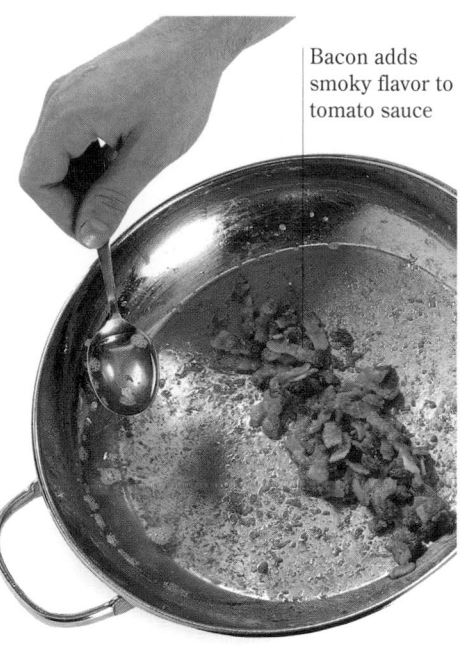

Bacon adds smoky flavor to tomato sauce

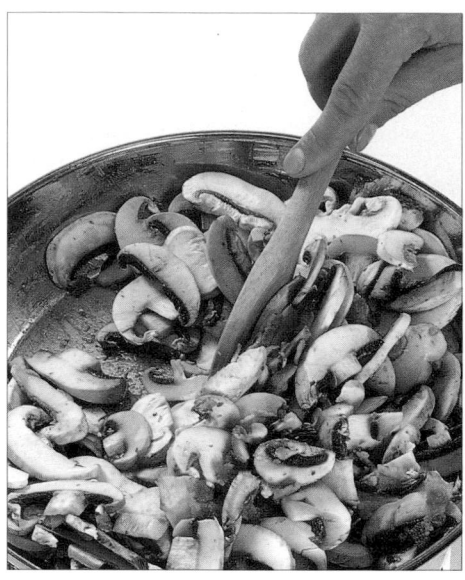

7 Transfer the bacon strips to the frying pan. Fry over low heat, stirring occasionally, until the bacon is lightly browned and the fat is rendered (melted), 5–7 minutes.

8 Spoon off most of the fat, leaving about 3 tbsp in which to sauté the mushrooms.

9 Increase the heat, add the sliced mushrooms to the pan. Cook, stirring with the wooden spoon, until mushrooms have softened and most of the liquid has evaporated, 3–5 minutes.

10 Add the garlic, chili pepper, oregano, chopped tomatoes with any juice, salt, and pepper. Bring to a boil, cover with a lid, and simmer, stirring occasionally, until the sauce is thick and rich, 25–30 minutes.

Fresh tomatoes will cook down to rich pulp

11 If necessary to thicken the sauce, continue to cook, without the lid, a few minutes longer. Taste the sauce for seasoning.

2 COOK THE QUILLS; FINISH THE DISH

2 Drain the quills in the colander and rinse with hot water to wash away any starch. Drain the quills again thoroughly.

🍽 TO SERVE

Transfer the quills to a warmed serving bowl and add the butter. Toss together with 2 large forks until well coated. Spoon over the sauce, and half of the grated cheese. Toss together, then sprinkle over a little more cheese and garnish with the reserved oregano leaves. Serve immediately, with the remaining cheese.

1 Fill the large pot with cold water, bring to a boil, and add 1 tbsp salt. Then add the quills. Simmer until *al dente*, tender but still chewy, 5–8 minutes, stirring occasionally.

Quill-shaped pasta holds plenty of sauce

SPAGHETTI WITH TOMATO AND CHILI SAUCE

Spaghetti alla Satana *is a perfect description for this dish, which is even spicier than* Penne all'Arrabbiata.

1 Omit the bacon, mushrooms, and oregano from the main recipe. Peel, seed, and chop 3 lb plum or medium tomatoes, as directed.

2 Chop 2 fresh or dried red chili peppers, discarding the seeds. Peel and chop 4 garlic cloves.

3 Heat 3 tbsp olive oil in a frying pan, add the chopped chili peppers and garlic, and sauté just until fragrant, about 30 seconds.

4 Add the chopped tomatoes, salt, and pepper and continue as directed.

5 Cook 1 lb dried spaghetti as for the quills. Drain and rinse the spaghetti, then toss with the sauce until thoroughly coated.

6 Serve on warmed individual plates, sprinkled with Parmesan cheese.

Tomato sauce can be made extra spicy by adding more chili pepper

BAKED RIGATONI WITH MEATBALLS

Timballo di Rigatoni

EQUIPMENT

food processor †

colander

slotted spoon

metal spatula

chef's knife

large frying pan

pastry brush

small knife

large metal spoon

bowls

wooden spoon

grater

large saucepans

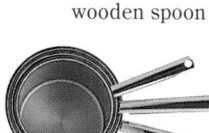

chopping board

2-quart soufflé dish

rubber spatula

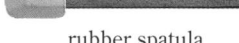

† blender can also be used

In this family favorite, rigatoni and tomato-basil sauce are embellished with small meatballs, then baked with a topping of Parmesan cheese. Italians like to use finger-length macaroni called mezzani, *but other tubular pasta, such as penne or short macaroni, are fine alternatives.*

GETTING AHEAD

The pasta can be baked 1 day ahead and kept refrigerated. Reheat it in a 375°F oven, 15–20 minutes before serving.

SHOPPING LIST

3	garlic cloves ✓
1	medium bunch of fresh basil
3 lb	fresh plum tomatoes
	salt and pepper ✓
3/4 lb	tubular pasta (rigatoni, penne, macaroni)
	For the meatballs
3–5	sprigs of flat-leaf parsley
1 lb	lean ground beef
1 cup	freshly grated Parmesan cheese
	juice of 1/2 lemon
1	egg
3 tbsp	olive oil, more for soufflé dish

INGREDIENTS

tubular pasta

Parmesan cheese

lemon juice

fresh basil

ground beef

plum tomatoes †

flat-leaf parsley ‡

garlic cloves

egg

olive oil

† medium tomatoes or 28 oz canned plum tomatoes can also be used

‡ curly parsley can also be used

ORDER OF WORK

1 MAKE THE TOMATO-BASIL SAUCE

2 MAKE THE MEATBALLS

3 COOK, ASSEMBLE, AND BAKE THE RIGATONI

1 MAKE THE TOMATO-BASIL SAUCE

1 Separate the garlic cloves from the bulb. Peel and finely chop the garlic (see box, page 42). Chop the basil leaves (see box, right).

2 Cut the cores from fresh tomatoes and score an "x" on the base of each with the tip of the small knife. Immerse them, a few at a time, in a saucepan of boiling water until the skins start to split, 8–15 seconds, depending on their ripeness.

Tomatoes immersed in cold water quickly become cool enough to handle

Tomato skins peel off easily after scalding

3 Using the slotted spoon, transfer the tomatoes at once to a bowl of cold water. When they are cold, peel off the skins. Cut the tomatoes crosswise in half, squeeze out the seeds, then coarsely chop each half. If using canned tomatoes, chop them, reserving their juice.

HOW TO CHOP HERBS

Basil, parsley, dill, chives, rosemary, and tarragon are herbs that are usually chopped before being added to other ingredients. Do not chop delicate herbs like basil too finely because they bruise easily.

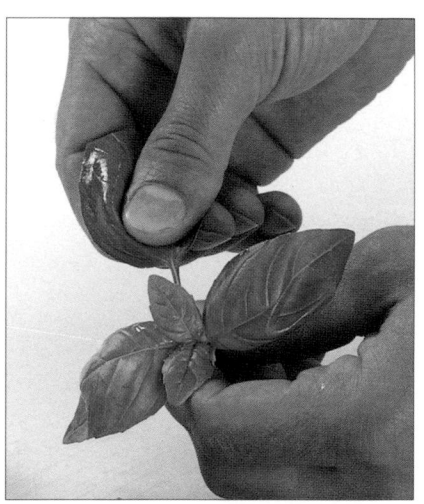

1 Strip the leaves or sprigs from the stems. Pile the leaves or sprigs on a chopping board.

Chop basil leaves coarsely to avoid bruising them

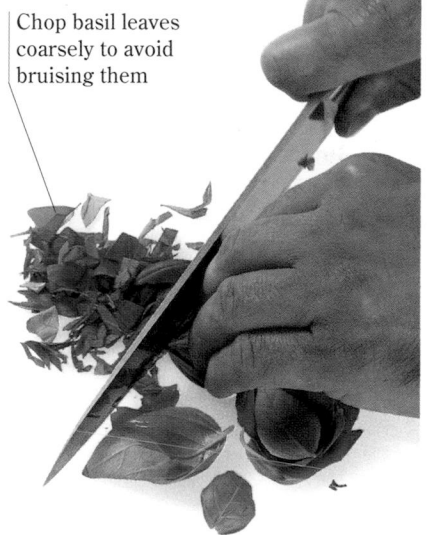

2 With a chef's knife, cut the herbs into small pieces. Holding the tip of the blade against the board and rocking the knife back and forth, chop until the herbs are coarse or fine, as you wish.

ANNE SAYS
"Make sure that your knife is very sharp, otherwise you will bruise the herbs rather than cut them."

4 Put the tomatoes, with any juice, in the frying pan and add two-thirds of the garlic, the basil, and a pinch of salt.

ANNE SAYS
"In winter months, canned tomatoes often have more flavor than fresh ones, and may be substituted for them in this dish."

Tomatoes are rich red in color, indicating ripeness and flavor

Chopped fresh basil enlivens tomato sauce

Fresh garlic adds pungency to sauce

5 Cook over medium heat, stirring occasionally, until slightly thickened, 10–12 minutes; there should be some liquid left in the pan.

6 Transfer to the food processor and purée the sauce. Season to taste with salt and pepper, and set aside. Wipe the frying pan clean.

HOW TO PEEL AND CHOP GARLIC

The strength of garlic varies with its age and dryness; use more when it is very fresh.

1 To peel a garlic clove, lightly crush it with the flat side of a chef's knife to loosen the skin.

2 Peel the skin from the garlic clove with your fingers and discard. Set the flat side of the chef's knife on top of the garlic clove and strike it firmly with your fist.

3 Finely chop the garlic clove with the chef's knife, rocking the blade back and forth.

2 MAKE THE MEATBALLS

1 Strip the parsley leaves from the stems and chop them, using the chef's knife. Put the ground beef, one-quarter of the Parmesan cheese, the chopped parsley leaves, remaining garlic, lemon juice, salt, and pepper in a bowl. Add the egg.

2 Mix all the ingredients in the bowl with your hands until they are thoroughly combined.

ANNE SAYS
"Hands make the best tools for mixing, but you can use a wooden spoon."

3 Test the mixture for seasoning: heat 1 tbsp oil in the frying pan, add a small spoonful of meatball mixture, and fry until brown on both sides. Taste, and adjust the seasoning of the remaining mixture, if necessary.

4 Shape the mixture into meatballs about 3/4 inch in diameter, wetting the palms of your hands so shaping the meat mixture is easier.

5 Heat the remaining oil in the frying pan. Add the meatballs, making sure they are not crowded in the pan. If necessary, fry them in batches.

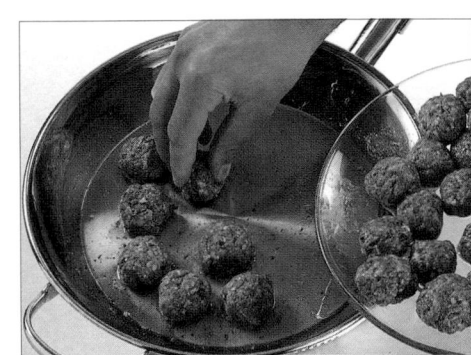

6 Fry the meatballs briskly, turning them with the metal spatula, until they are brown on the outside and still pink inside, 2–4 minutes. Transfer them to a large plate with the slotted spoon, and set aside.

Turn meatballs when browned on one side

! TAKE CARE !
If the oil is not hot enough, the meatballs will stick.

3 COOK, ASSEMBLE, AND BAKE THE RIGATONI

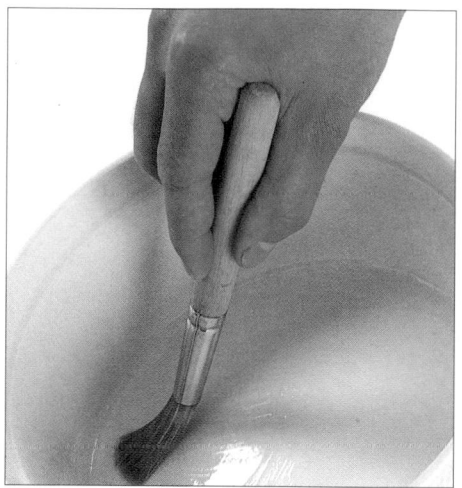

1 Heat the oven to 375°F. Brush the inside of the soufflé dish lightly with a little olive oil.

2 Fill a large saucepan with water, bring to a boil, and add 1 tbsp salt. Add the pasta to the pan and simmer until *al dente*, tender but still chewy, 8–10 minutes, or according to package directions. Stir the pasta occasionally to keep from sticking.

Rinse pasta with hot water so starch is washed away and pasta remains hot

Shake colander while rinsing so water drains away completely

3 Drain the pasta in the colander, rinse with hot water, and drain again thoroughly.

ANNE SAYS
"Rinsing washes away excess starch."

Stir gently so pasta does not break up

4 Return the rinsed and drained pasta to the saucepan and pour in the tomato-basil sauce.

5 Gently stir the pasta and sauce together until the pasta is well coated with the sauce.

6 Spoon about one-third of the pasta and sauce into the prepared soufflé dish and level the surface.

7 Spoon half of the meatballs on top. Sprinkle with one-third of the remaining Parmesan cheese. Top with half of the remaining pasta then the rest of the meatballs. Sprinkle with half of the remaining Parmesan.

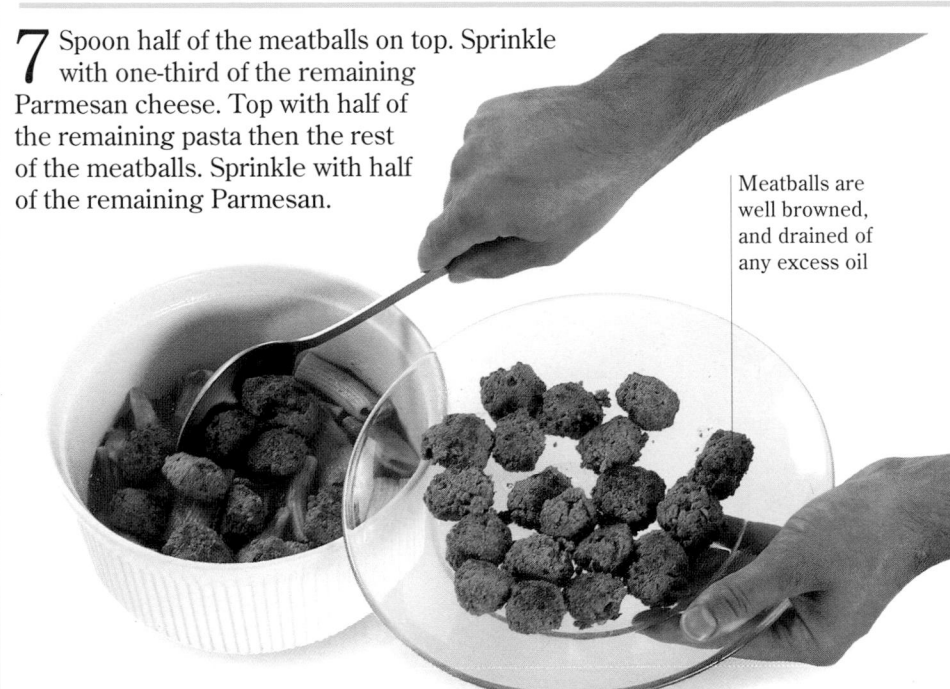

Meatballs are well browned, and drained of any excess oil

8 Add the remaining pasta and cover it with the rest of the Parmesan cheese. Bake the timballo in the heated oven until very hot and the top is browned, 30–40 minutes. Let stand so the flavors blend together, about 15 minutes.

¶◎¶ TO SERVE
Sprinkle with a little shredded basil, if you like, and serve warm.

Plump rigatoni
hides a surprise layer of meatballs underneath

Shreds of basil
hint at flavor in tomato sauce

Parmesan cheese
makes golden topping for timballo

BAKED ZITI WITH MOZZARELLA AND OLIVES

In this variation of baked rigatoni, Timballo di Ziti, *chunks of mozzarella cheese and black olives replace the meatballs, and anchovies spice the tomato sauce.*

1 Chop 8 anchovy fillets. Make the tomato sauce as directed in the main recipe, adding the chopped anchovies to the tomatoes with the garlic. Omit the basil.
2 Omit the meatballs. Pit 1 cup Gaeta or oil-cured black olives. Cut ½ lb mozzarella cheese into small cubes. Oil the soufflé dish.
3 Cook ¾ lb ziti as for the pasta in the main recipe, and drain thoroughly.
4 Layer the pasta, tomato sauce, and fillings as directed, with the pitted olives in place of the meatballs and the mozzarella cubes in place of the Parmesan cheese.
5 Bake as directed until very hot and the cheese is melted, 20–25 minutes.
6 Serve on warmed individual plates.

FRESH POLENTA WITH VEGETABLE STEW

Polenta con Fricandò

 SERVES 6–8 WORK TIME 35–40 MINUTES COOKING TIME 35–50 MINUTES

EQUIPMENT

large sauté pan

colander

paper towels

bowl

saucepans

wooden spoon

whisk

slotted spoon

chef's knife

chopping board

small knife

In Italy, this creamy polenta topped with a stew of eggplant, zucchini, bell peppers, tomatoes, and onions would be served at the start of a meal, but it is substantial enough to act as a vegetarian main course, accompanied by a green salad.

GETTING AHEAD

The vegetable stew can be made up to 1 day ahead and refrigerated; the flavor will mellow. Reheat the stew on top of the stove and cook the polenta just before serving.

SHOPPING LIST

2 quarts	water
1 tbsp	salt
3 cups	yellow cornmeal
3 tbsp	butter
	For the vegetable stew
2	medium eggplant, total weight about 1 lb
2	medium zucchini, total weight about 1 lb
	salt and pepper
3	onions
4	garlic cloves
2	red bell peppers
1 lb	fresh plum tomatoes
1	medium bunch of fresh basil
¼ cup	olive oil, more if needed

INGREDIENTS

zucchini

yellow cornmeal

red bell peppers

eggplant

butter

onions

garlic cloves

plum tomatoes†

olive oil

fresh basil

† medium tomatoes or 14 oz canned plum tomatoes can also be used

ORDER OF WORK

1 PREPARE THE VEGETABLES

2 COOK THE VEGETABLE STEW

3 COOK THE POLENTA

1 PREPARE THE VEGETABLES

Diagonal slices look attractive

1 Trim the ends of the eggplant and cut lengthwise in half, then cut each half into 6–7 lengthwise strips. Bunch the strips together and cut them across into 1-inch chunks.

2 Trim the zucchini and cut them lengthwise in half. Cut each half diagonally into ½-inch slices.

3 Put the eggplant and zucchini on a large plate or tray and sprinkle them generously with salt. Let stand to draw out the bitter juices, 30 minutes.

When slicing, guide knife blade with curled fingers of other hand

4 Meanwhile, peel the onions, leaving a little of the root attached, and cut lengthwise in half. Lay each half flat and cut across into medium slices. Set the flat side of the chef's knife on top of each garlic clove and strike it with your fist. Discard the skins and finely chop the garlic.

5 With the small knife, cut around the bell pepper cores, twist, and pull them out. Halve the peppers and scrape out the seeds. Cut away the white ribs on the inside. Set each pepper half cut-side down, flatten with the heel of your hand, and slice lengthwise into strips.

6 Peel, seed, and coarsely chop the fresh tomatoes (see box, page 48). If using canned tomatoes, drain them, reserving the juice, and chop them. Strip the basil leaves from the stems, reserving 6–8 sprigs for decoration, and pile them on the chopping board. With the chef's knife, coarsely chop the basil leaves.

7 Rinse the eggplant and zucchini with cold water and pat dry with paper towels.

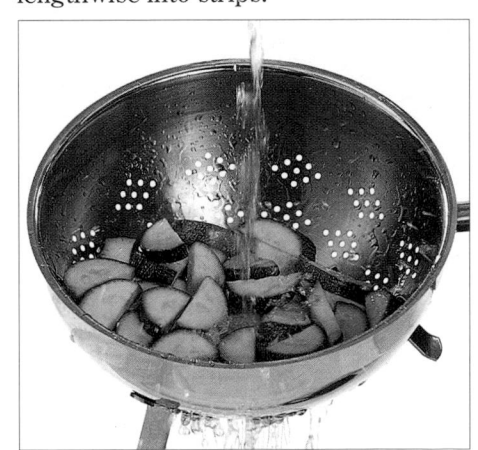

2 COOK THE VEGETABLE STEW

Scatter zucchini slices into pan

1 Heat the olive oil in the sauté pan. Add the onions and garlic, and cook, stirring, until soft but not brown, 3–5 minutes. Stir in the bell pepper slices and then the eggplant chunks, and cook 2–3 minutes longer.

2 Add the zucchini and continue cooking, stirring often, until the vegetables are just tender, 7–10 minutes. Add more oil if needed. Stir in the tomatoes with any juice, salt, and pepper. Simmer, stirring occasionally, until thickened, 12–15 minutes.

HOW TO PEEL, SEED, AND CHOP TOMATOES

Tomatoes are often peeled and seeded before they are chopped so they can be cooked to a purée. The technique is the same, for plum or other tomatoes.

1 Cut the cores from the tomatoes and score an "x" on the base of each tomato with the tip of a small knife.

2 Immerse the tomatoes in a pan of boiling water until the skins start to split, 8–15 seconds, depending on their ripeness. Using a slotted spoon, transfer the tomatoes at once to a bowl of cold water.

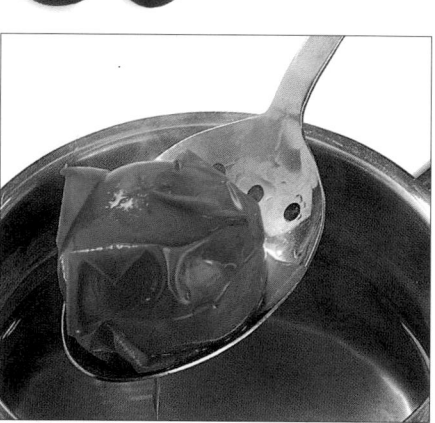

3 When the tomatoes are cool enough to handle, peel the skin off each one, using the small knife.

4 With a chef's knife, cut the tomatoes crosswise in half. Squeeze out the seeds, then coarsely chop each half.

Hold tip of blade and rock handle up and down

3 COOK THE POLENTA

1 Bring the water to a boil in a large saucepan and add the salt. Over medium heat, slowly whisk in the cornmeal in a thin, steady stream. Whisk constantly to avoid lumps.

2 Cook the cornmeal, stirring occasionally, until it is thick enough to hold a shape and pulls away from the side of the pan, 15–20 minutes. Beat in the butter.

ANNE SAYS
"*Taste the polenta; when done it should be just firm enough to hold a shape, with no taste of uncooked cornmeal.*"

🍽 TO SERVE

If necessary, reheat the vegetable stew. Stir in most of the chopped basil and taste for seasoning. Spoon the polenta onto warmed plates, top with stew, and sprinkle with the remaining chopped basil. Decorate with the reserved basil sprigs.

Basil sprig is bright, aromatic decoration

Red bell peppers accent vegetable stew

GRILLED POLENTA WITH VEGETABLE STEW

Here polenta squares, Quadrati di Polenta, *are grilled on the barbecue.*

1 Prepare the polenta as directed in the main recipe, omitting the butter.
2 Sprinkle a baking sheet with water. Using a metal spatula, spread the polenta evenly on the baking sheet in a 1/2-inch layer and cool completely.
3 Prepare the vegetable stew as directed, substituting 1 red, 1 green, and 1 yellow bell pepper for the 2 red bell peppers.
4 Heat the barbecue grill. Add salt and plenty of pepper to 1/4 cup olive oil.
5 Cut the polenta into sixteen 3-inch squares. Brush with the seasoned oil. Set the squares, oiled-side down, on the rack, and grill 4 inches from the heat, 2–3 minutes, until the grill marks show. Rotate the squares 45° and continue grilling so the marks form diamonds. Turn over and grill on the other side. Brush with oil during cooking and brush again after cooking.
6 Serve the polenta squares with the vegetable stew on warmed individual plates, sprinkled with chopped basil.

ANNE SAYS
"*If you don't have a grill, you can also pan-fry the polenta squares in the seasoned oil: heat the oil in a large skillet or frying pan. Add the squares in batches and fry until golden, 2–3 minutes on each side, adding more oil as necessary.*"

Spinach and Potato Gnocchi in Tomato-Cream Sauce

Gnocchi Verdi al Sugo di Pomodoro e Panna

 Serves 6–8 Work Time 50–55 minutes Cooking Time 30–40 minutes

Equipment

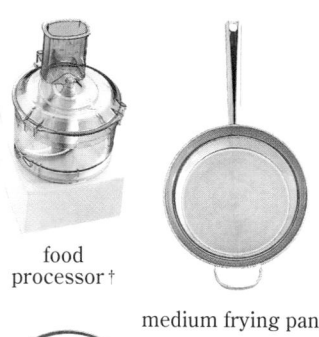

food processor †

medium frying pan

chef's knife

slotted spoon

bowls

wooden spoon

rubber spatula

small knife

vegetable peeler

paper towels

baking dish

colander

baking sheet

saucepans, 1 with lid

potato masher ‡

† blender can also be used
‡ potato ricer can also be used

I find that dumplings made only with flour can be heavy, but potato gnocchi never fail to please. Hearty, but not leaden, they are flavored here with spinach, and served in a fresh tomato and cream sauce. The shape of the gnocchi ensures that they cook evenly and hold the sauce well.

Getting Ahead

The gnocchi and tomato-cream sauce can both be made up to 1 day ahead and kept separately, tightly covered, in the refrigerator. Add the cream to the sauce and bake the gnocchi just before serving.

Shopping List

2 lb	baking potatoes
½ lb	fresh or 5 oz defrosted spinach
1 cup	flour, more if needed
	For the tomato-cream sauce
1	small onion
1	medium carrot
1	celery stalk
3 lb	fresh plum tomatoes
3 tbsp	butter, more for baking dish
	salt and pepper
1 cup	heavy cream
1	pinch of ground nutmeg

Ingredients

plum tomatoes †

baking potatoes

fresh spinach

onion

carrot

celery

butter

ground nutmeg

flour

heavy cream

† medium tomatoes or 28 oz canned plum tomatoes can also be used

Order of Work

1 Make the Tomato-Cream Sauce

2 Make the Spinach and Potato Gnocchi

3 Cook and Finish the Gnocchi

1 MAKE THE TOMATO-CREAM SAUCE

Guide blade with your knuckles

1 Peel the onion, leaving a little of the root attached, and cut it lengthwise in half. Lay each half flat on a chopping board and slice horizontally toward the root, leaving the slices attached at the root end, and then slice vertically, again leaving the root end uncut. Cut across to make dice.

2 Peel and trim the carrot, cut it crosswise in half, then cut it vertically into ¹/₄-inch slices. Stack the slices and cut into ¹/₄-inch strips. Gather the strips together in a pile and cut crosswise to produce dice.

3 Cut the celery stalk lengthwise into ¹/₄-inch strips, then gather the strips together in a pile and cut crosswise to make small dice.

ANNE SAYS
"You can chop all the vegetables together in the food processor."

4 Cut the cores from fresh tomatoes and score an "x" on the base of each with the tip of a knife. Immerse the tomatoes in a large saucepan of boiling water until the skins start to split, 8–15 seconds, depending on their ripeness. Using the slotted spoon, transfer them at once to a bowl of cold water. When cold, peel off the skins.

Remove tomatoes from boiling water as soon as skins start to split so they do not cook

Tomatoes immersed in cold water will quickly become cool enough to handle

5 Cut the tomatoes crosswise in half, squeeze out the seeds, and chop coarsely. If using canned tomatoes, chop them, reserving the juice.

6 Melt the butter in the frying pan. Add the chopped onion, carrot, and celery, and cook over medium heat, stirring, until tender, 7–10 minutes.

7 Add the tomatoes to the pan with any juice, salt, and pepper, and simmer, stirring occasionally, until thick, 25–35 minutes. Meanwhile, make the gnocchi.

8 Transfer the tomato sauce to the food processor and purée until smooth. Alternatively, work it through a strainer. Wipe the frying pan clean.

Most, but not all, liquid should have evaporated from tomato mixture

2 MAKE THE SPINACH AND POTATO GNOCCHI

2 Simmer the potatoes until very tender when pierced with the tip of the small knife, 15–20 minutes. Drain the potatoes – they must be very dry.

ANNE SAYS
"If the potatoes seem moist, spread them on a baking sheet and let dry in a low oven with the door open, 5–10 minutes."

1 Peel the potatoes and cut each one into several pieces. Put them in a medium saucepan of cold salted water, cover, and bring to a boil.

3 Mash the dry potatoes in the pan with the potato masher. Alternatively, work them through a potato ricer into a bowl.

Add spinach to pan in handfuls

Cook spinach in boiling water to preserve color and nutrients

4 Prepare the fresh spinach, if using: discard the tough ribs and stems from the spinach, then wash the leaves under cold water.

5 Bring another saucepan of cold salted water to a boil. Add the spinach and simmer until tender, 1–2 minutes. Drain the spinach in the colander, rinse with cold water, and drain again.

Squeezing spinach in your fist is best way to remove excess water

6 Squeeze the cooked fresh spinach or defrosted spinach, in your fist to remove all excess water. Purée the spinach in the food processor, or chop finely.

7 Add the spinach to the mashed potatoes with the flour, salt, and pepper, and mix together well with the wooden spoon. Taste for seasoning.

8 Transfer to a lightly floured work surface and knead lightly to form a dough, working in a little more flour to bind the mixture, if necessary.

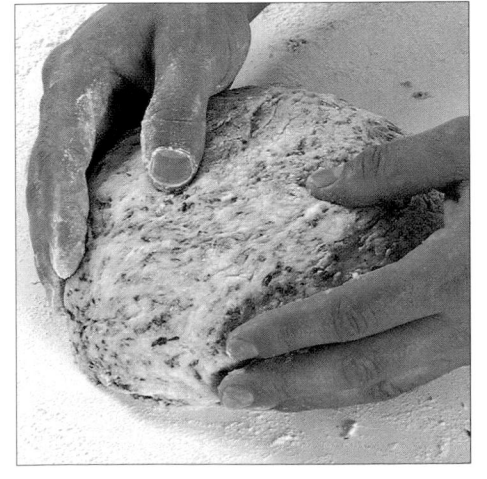

9 To test the consistency, roll a 3/4-inch ball of dough, drop it into a saucepan of simmering water, and cook until it floats to the surface. If the gnocchi falls apart, add about 2 tbsp more flour to the dough, then test again. If the gnocchi does not fall apart, shape the remaining dough.

Cut gnocchi all the same size so they cook evenly

10 Divide the dough into 12 equal pieces. Lightly flour your hands and roll each piece of dough into a long cylinder about $1/2$ inch in diameter. Then cut each cylinder crosswise into logs $3/4$-inch long.

11 Lightly flour the baking sheet. Hold a fork in one hand with the concave side toward you and the tines pointing horizontally. With the thumb of your other hand, roll each piece of dough from the inside curve of the fork to the tips of the prongs, and let it drop onto the baking sheet.

3 COOK AND FINISH THE GNOCCHI

1 Heat the oven to 425°F. Butter the baking dish. Heat a large saucepan of salted water to boiling. Add about one-quarter of the gnocchi. Cook until they float to the surface, 1–2 minutes.

! TAKE CARE !
Stir the gnocchi occasionally to make sure they do not stick.

2 Transfer the gnocchi to drain on paper towels, then place in the baking dish. Continue cooking the gnocchi in batches.

Protect your fingers with a folded cloth or pot holder

Swirl cream into tomato sauce until evenly blended

3 Reheat the tomato sauce in the frying pan, remove from heat and stir in the cream. Season the sauce to taste with salt, pepper, and ground nutmeg.

Coat gnocchi completely with sauce so they do not dry out during baking

4 Spoon the sauce evenly over the gnocchi in the baking dish. Bake the gnocchi in the heated oven until very hot and starting to brown, 5–7 minutes. Serve immediately, sprinkled with chopped flat-leaf parsley, if you like.

Tomato-cream sauce makes a colorful contrast to spinach gnocchi

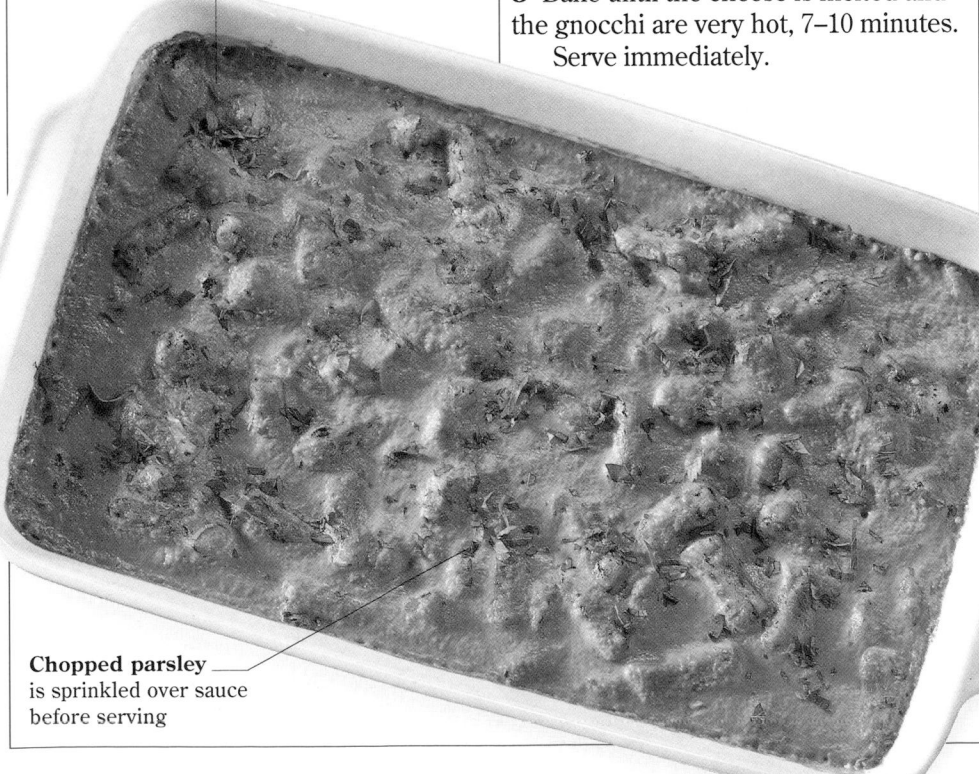

Chopped parsley is sprinkled over sauce before serving

VARIATION

SPINACH AND POTATO GNOCCHI WITH CHEESE

1 Omit the tomato-cream sauce. Make and cook the spinach gnocchi as directed in the main recipe.
2 Heat the oven to 425°F. Arrange half of the gnocchi in a single layer on the bottom of a buttered large baking dish.
3 Slice $1/2$ lb fontina, mozzarella, or Gruyère cheese very thinly; melt $1/4$ cup butter. Scatter half of the cheese on the gnocchi and spoon on half of the butter. Sprinkle with salt and pepper.
4 Spread the gnocchi on top, then the remaining cheese and melted butter. Season again.
5 Bake until the cheese is melted and the gnocchi are very hot, 7–10 minutes. Serve immediately.

VARIATION

PLAIN GNOCCHI WITH GORGONZOLA SAUCE

A thyme-scented, creamy Gorgonzola sauce tops plain gnocchi here.

1 Make plain gnocchi as directed in the main recipe, omitting the spinach and using $3/4$ cup flour for the dough. Cover the gnocchi and keep them warm in a low oven.
2 Omit the tomato-cream sauce and make a Gorgonzola sauce: cut 6 oz Gorgonzola or other blue cheese into small cubes.
3 Strip the leaves from 10–12 sprigs of fresh thyme and pile them on a chopping board. With a chef's knife, finely chop the leaves.
4 Melt 3 tbsp butter in a large saucepan and stir in $3/4$ cup heavy cream. Add the Gorgonzola, chopped thyme, salt, and pepper, and heat gently, stirring, until the cheese is melted. Do not let boil.
5 Add the sauce to the gnocchi and taste for seasoning.
6 Spoon the gnocchi with Gorgonzola sauce onto warmed individual plates and decorate with a thyme sprig. If you like, sprinkle with $1/4$ cup freshly grated Parmesan cheese.

ANNE SAYS
"If you prefer a thicker cheese sauce, let the sauce cool slightly before tossing it with the gnocchi."

SOLE FILLETS MARINATED IN VINEGAR

Sfogi in Saor

EQUIPMENT

salad spinner

chef's knife

large frying pan

wooden spoon

metal spatula

paper towels

whisk

bowls

small knife

slotted spatula

non-metallic baking dish

plastic wrap

aluminum foil

chopping board

Before the days of refrigeration, pickling was a common method of preserving. This delicious sole recipe has survived despite modern appliances. The quantity given here serves 4 as a main course, 6 as an appetizer.

GETTING AHEAD

The fish can be cooked and covered with the marinade up to 1 day ahead. Keep it, tightly covered, in the refrigerator.

*plus 12–24 hours marinating time

SHOPPING LIST

1	large onion
6 tbsp	olive oil
	salt and pepper
1 cup	red wine vinegar
1/4 cup	dark raisins
1 lb	sole fillets
1/4 cup	flour
1/4 cup	pine nuts
	For the salad
1/2 lb	arugula
	juice of 1/2 orange
3 tbsp	olive oil

INGREDIENTS

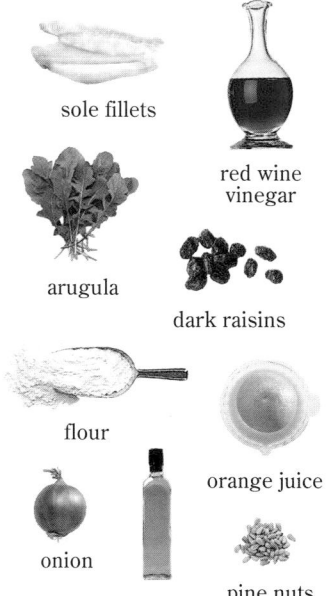

sole fillets

red wine vinegar

arugula

dark raisins

flour

orange juice

onion

olive oil

pine nuts

ANNE SAYS

"If you prefer a milder marinade, use half of the quantity of vinegar and an equal amount of white wine."

ORDER OF WORK

1 PREPARE THE MARINADE

2 COOK AND MARINATE THE FISH

3 PREPARE THE SALAD AND SERVE THE SOLE

1 PREPARE THE MARINADE

1 Peel the onion, leaving a little of the root attached, and cut lengthwise in half through root and stem.

Small knife makes peeling easy

ANNE SAYS
"*Onions should be firm, with no sign of sprouting, and no black or powdery spots.*"

2 Lay each onion half flat on the chopping board and cut across into thin slices.

3 Heat one-third of the oil in the large frying pan. Add the onion slices with a little salt and pepper, cover with foil, and cook over low heat, stirring occasionally, until very soft, 15–20 minutes.

Sweetness of raisins counterbalances sharpness of vinegar

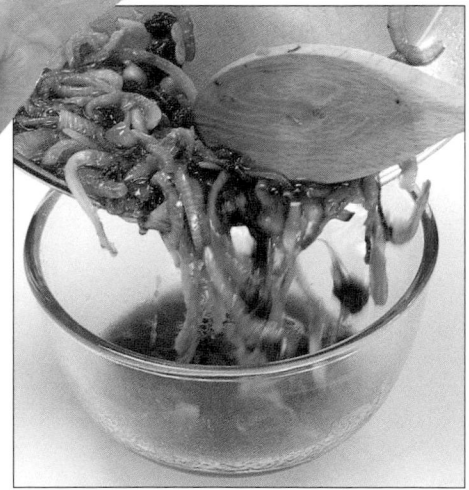

4 Remove the foil from the frying pan, increase the heat, and continue cooking the onion slices until they are lightly browned and caramelized, 3–5 minutes.

5 Add the red wine vinegar and the raisins to the onions. Heat to boiling, and boil 2 minutes.

6 Transfer the vinegar mixture from the frying pan to a bowl; set aside while preparing the fish.

2 COOK AND MARINATE THE FISH

Sole has delicate,
fine-textured
flesh

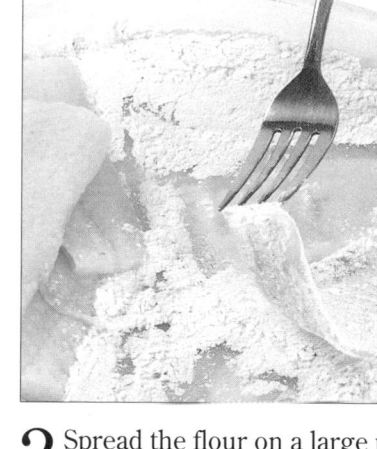

Dry fish with paper
towels so flour
does not clog
when coating

1 Rinse the sole fillets
and pat dry with paper
towels. With the chef's knife,
cut the fillets crosswise into pieces
about 2 inches wide.

2 Spread the flour on a large plate
and season with salt and pepper.
Add some of the fish pieces and, with a
fork, turn the pieces in the seasoned
flour so they are evenly coated.
Transfer to a second plate and coat the
remaining fish pieces.

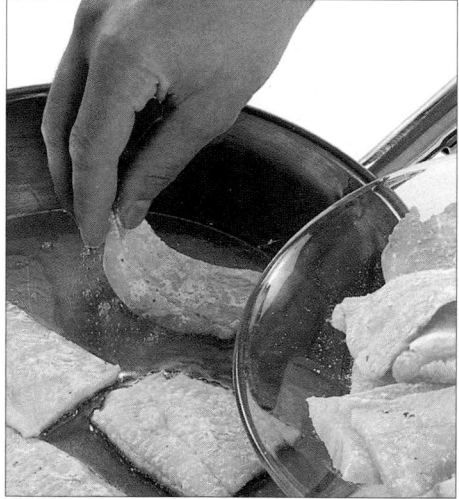

ANNE SAYS
"*If necessary, cook the fish
in batches so the pan is not
crowded, adding more oil
when required.*"

3 Heat the remaining oil and add the
sole pieces. Cook over medium-
high heat until browned, 1–2 minutes.

4 Turn the sole
pieces, and pan-
fry until the flesh just
flakes when tested with a
fork, 1–2 minutes longer.
Drain the fish on paper towels
and let cool completely.

Test fish as soon
as it loses its transparent
appearance because it
quickly overcooks

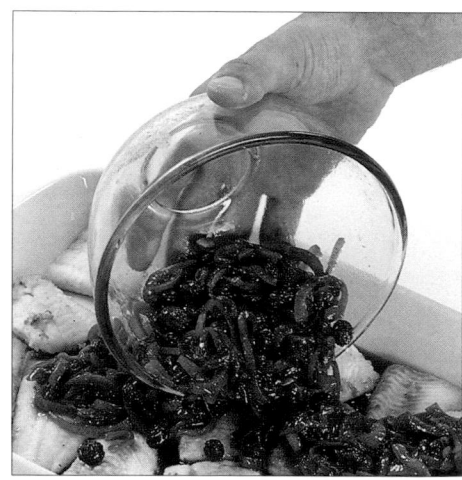

5 Spread the sole pieces in the
baking dish and cover them with
the vinegar mixture.

6 Sprinkle with the pine nuts.
Cover tightly and leave to
marinate in the refrigerator,
12 hours, or up to 24 hours.

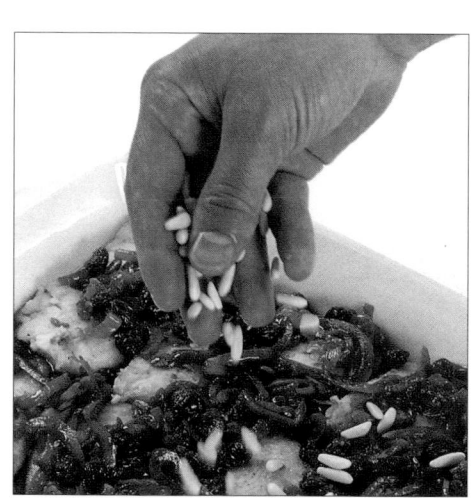

3 PREPARE THE SALAD AND SERVE THE SOLE

1 Discard the tough stems from the arugula and wash the leaves in plenty of cold water. Dry the leaves in the salad spinner or on a dish towel.

2 Pour the orange juice into a large bowl and whisk in salt and pepper to taste. Gradually whisk in the oil so the vinaigrette emulsifies and thickens slightly. Taste for seasoning.

🍴 TO SERVE

Remove the fish from the refrigerator and allow it to come to room temperature, about 1 hour. Add the arugula to the dressing and toss. Arrange the arugula on a serving platter, place the pieces of sole on top, and spoon on the marinade.

Crisp, bitter arugula leaves and crunchy nuts complement sweet-and-sour fish

Small pieces of fish absorb flavor from marinade

SOLE FILLETS MARINATED WITH VINEGAR AND SAFFRON

Saffron adds an attractive color to the pickling liquid in Pesce a Scapece.

1 Omit the onion, raisins, and pine nuts from the main recipe. Peel and chop 2 garlic cloves: set the flat side of a chef's knife on top of each garlic clove and strike it with your fist. Discard the skins and finely chop the garlic.

2 Prepare and fry the sole pieces as directed in the main recipe, and spread them in the baking dish.

3 Put ³/₄ cup white wine vinegar and a large pinch of saffron in a small pan. Bring to a boil, then let cool.

4 Whisk in the chopped garlic and ¹/₃ cup olive oil. Pour this marinade over the sole pieces and season with plenty of black pepper. Cover tightly, and leave to marinate in the refrigerator, as directed.

5 Remove the fish from the refrigerator, and allow to come to room temperature.

6 Meanwhile, prepare the arugula and orange dressing as directed, and toss the leaves in the dressing.

7 Arrange the salad leaves on individual plates with the pieces of fish on top. Decorate with a twisted lemon slice, if you like.

ANNE SAYS

"If your vinegar is very acidic, use only ¹/₂ cup vinegar and add ¹/₄ cup water."

BEEF BRAISED IN RED WINE

Stufato di Manzo al Barbera

🍽 SERVES 6   🥣 WORK TIME 15–20 MINUTES   ♨ COOKING TIME 4–4½ HOURS

EQUIPMENT

large flameproof casserole
with lid

aluminum foil

chopping board

wooden spoons

2-pronged fork

vegetable peeler

chef's knife

small knife

ANNE SAYS
"*A thick earthenware casserole that is glazed on the inside is traditionally used because it allows the beef to cook slowly and evenly. The fragrant steam produced during cooking condenses on the lid and drips back onto the meat, basting it and keeping it moist.*"

A beef roast braised in red wine is a favorite dish in northern Italy. Ovens did not find their way into many domestic Italian kitchens until after World War II, so Stufato was traditionally cooked on top of the stove. Barbera is the preferred wine but you can substitute any dry red. Gnocchi (see page 50), served in the wine sauce, is the perfect accompaniment, although braised carrots or leeks are also delicious.

GETTING AHEAD

The beef can be prepared up to 3 days ahead and kept, covered, in the refrigerator. Reheat it on top of the stove, stirring occasionally, before serving.

SHOPPING LIST

1	small carrot
1	celery stalk
1	small onion
1	beef chuck roast, weighing about 4 lb
2 tbsp	olive oil
2 cups	dry red wine
1 tbsp	tomato paste
2 cups	beef stock (see box, page 122), more if needed
2–3	sprigs of fresh thyme
	salt and pepper

INGREDIENTS

beef chuck roast

dry red wine

celery

fresh thyme

onion

tomato paste

carrot

olive oil

beef stock †

† water can also be used

ANNE SAYS
"*Barbera is the most widely produced wine of Piedmont. The best varieties will have a Denominazione di Origine Controllate (D.O.C.), but even these are everyday wines.*"

ORDER OF WORK

1 PREPARE THE VEGETABLES

2 COOK THE BEEF

1 PREPARE THE VEGETABLES

"Squared-off" carrot is easy to dice

1 Peel and trim the carrot. Cut it crosswise in half and square off the sides using the chef's knife. Cut the halves vertically into ¼-inch slices. Stack the slices and cut into ¼-inch strips. Gather the strips in a pile and cut crosswise to produce dice.

2 Peel the strings from the celery stalk with the vegetable peeler. Cut in half, then cut the halves lengthwise into ¼-inch strips. Gather the strips together in a pile and cut crosswise to make small dice. Chop the onion (see box, right).

2 COOK THE BEEF

Turning with spoons stops beef from being pierced and losing juices

1 Heat the oven to 300°F. With the chef's knife, trim any excess fat and sinew from the beef. Heat the oil in the flameproof casserole.

2 Add the beef and brown it well on all sides, turning it with 2 wooden spoons. Transfer the beef to a plate, and lower the heat to medium.

Hot oil sears beef, sealing in juices

HOW TO CHOP AN ONION

The size of dice when chopping an onion depends on the thickness of the initial slices. For a standard size, make slices about ¼-inch thick. For finely chopped onions, slice as thinly as possible.

1 Peel the onion and trim the top; leave a little of the root attached. Cut the onion lengthwise in half with a chef's knife.

2 Lay each onion half, cut-side down, on a chopping board. With the chef's knife, slice the onion half horizontally toward the root, leaving the slices attached at the root end.

3 Then slice vertically, again leaving the root end uncut. Finally, cut across the onion to make dice.

Wine dissolves caramelized meat juices

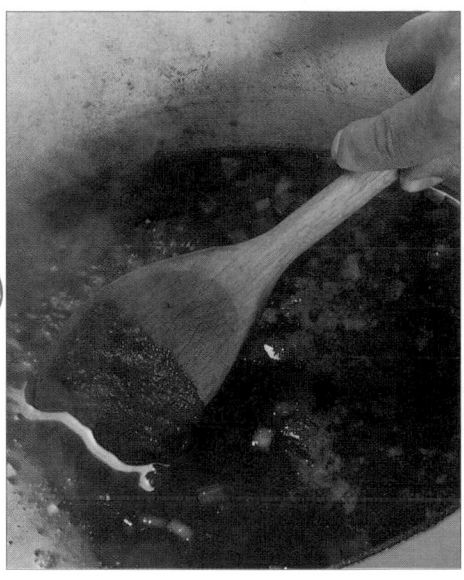

3 Add the chopped onion, carrot, and celery to the casserole and cook, stirring occasionally, until the vegetables are soft, 3–5 minutes.

4 Add the red wine to the casserole, stir to dissolve the pan juices, and bring the liquid to a boil.

5 Stir in the tomato paste until evenly blended. Return the beef to the casserole. Add enough beef stock to come halfway up the sides of the meat.

Cooking liquid should be simmering

6 Add the thyme sprigs and season with salt and pepper. Bring the liquid to a boil on top of the stove, then cover the casserole tightly.

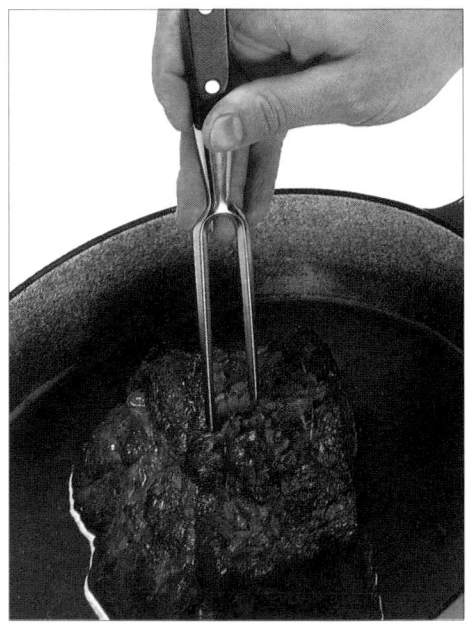

7 Cook in the heated oven until the meat is very tender when pierced with the 2-pronged fork, $4-4^1/_2$ hours. Turn the meat 3–4 times during cooking and add more stock if the casserole seems dry.

! TAKE CARE !
The cooking liquid should remain at a simmer, not boiling, so the beef does not cook too quickly.

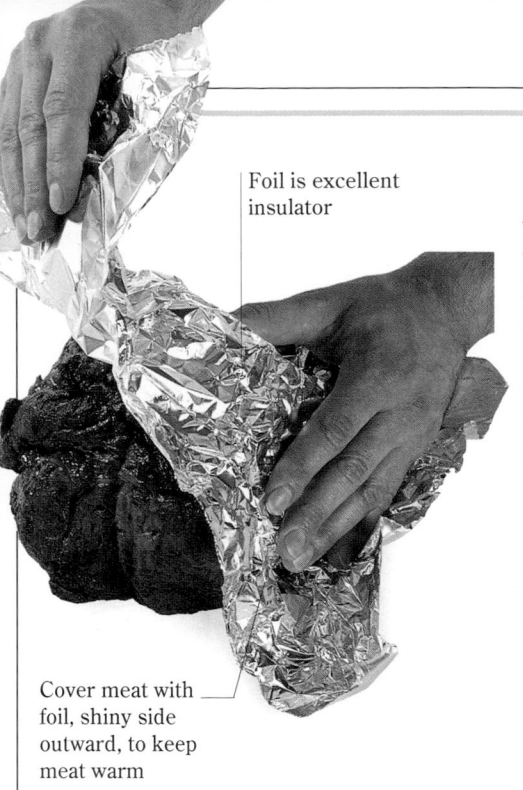

Foil is excellent insulator

Cover meat with foil, shiny side outward, to keep meat warm

¶◉¶   TO SERVE

Arrange the beef slices on warmed individual plates. If you like, serve the beef with gnocchi. Spoon a little cooking liquid over the beef and gnocchi and serve the rest separately.

8 Transfer the meat to the chopping board and cover with foil, to keep it warm. Boil the cooking liquid until thickened and reduced to about 1 cup. Discard the thyme sprigs and taste the cooking liquid for seasoning.

9 Using the chef's knife, carve the meat into neat slices on the chopping board.

Gnocchi is a perfect partner for beef braised in red wine

Cooking juices are dark and rich

V A R I A T I O N

BRAISED LAMB WITH POTATOES AND TOMATOES

Agnello al Forno con Patate e Pomodori – *lamb braised with potatoes and tomatoes – is popular in southern Italy.*

1 Trim 2 lb boneless leg of lamb and cut it into 1½-inch cubes. Chop the onion and carrot. Omit the celery.
2 Peel, seed, and coarsely chop ¾ lb ripe plum or medium tomatoes.
3 Peel 1 lb new potatoes.
4 Substitute ½ cup white wine for the red wine, and the same amount of fresh rosemary for the thyme sprigs. Omit the tomato paste and beef stock.
5 Brown the lamb cubes in a medium flameproof casserole, then sauté the onion and carrot as directed. Add the white wine and rosemary and boil until reduced by half.
6 Return the lamb cubes to the casserole, add the chopped tomatoes, and salt and pepper. Bring to a boil, cover, and simmer 30 minutes on top of the stove. Meanwhile, heat the oven to 300°F.
7 Transfer the casserole to the heated oven and cook the lamb 30 minutes. Add the potatoes and continue cooking, stirring occasionally, until the lamb cubes are tender, 1¼– 1¾ hours longer. Add water during cooking if the casserole becomes dry.
8 Taste the cooking liquid for seasoning. Spoon a little liquid over the lamb and serve with the potatoes.

MILANESE VEAL SCALOPPINE

Scaloppine alla Milanese

🍽 SERVES 6 🥄 WORK TIME 20–25 MINUTES 🍲 FRYING TIME 4–12 MINUTES*

EQUIPMENT

shallow dish

frying pans

wooden spoon

strainer

2-pronged fork

small knife

paper towels

bowl

chef's knife

rolling pin

parchment paper†

chopping board

† waxed paper or plastic wrap can also be used

In this northern Italian classic, veal slices are coated with breadcrumbs and cheese, and lightly pan-fried. The accompaniment of bell peppers sautéed in garlic and olive oil is a favorite of mine.

GETTING AHEAD

The veal scaloppine can be coated up to 4 hours ahead; keep them uncovered in the refrigerator.

*total frying time depends on size of frying pan

SHOPPING LIST

6	veal scaloppine, total weight about ³/₄ lb
¹/₄ cup	flour
	salt and pepper
2	eggs
¹/₂ cup	dry breadcrumbs
¹/₂ cup	freshly grated Parmesan cheese
1	lemon for garnish
2 tbsp	butter
2 tbsp	olive oil, more if needed
	For the sautéed bell peppers
1	garlic clove
7–10	sprigs of fresh oregano
1	small green bell pepper
1	small red bell pepper
2 tbsp	olive oil

INGREDIENTS

veal scaloppine

eggs

fresh oregano

garlic clove

olive oil

butter

green bell pepper

red bell pepper

lemon

flour

grated Parmesan cheese

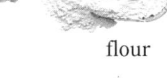

dry breadcrumbs

ORDER OF WORK

1 PREPARE THE VEAL SCALOPPINE

2 SAUTÉ THE BELL PEPPERS

3 MAKE THE GARNISH AND COOK THE VEAL

1 PREPARE THE VEAL SCALOPPINE

1 If necessary, flatten the veal: put 2 veal scaloppine between 2 sheets of parchment paper. Pound lightly to ⅛-inch thickness with the rolling pin. Repeat with the remaining slices.

Flatten veal carefully so holes do not form

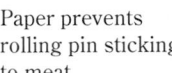

Paper prevents rolling pin sticking to meat

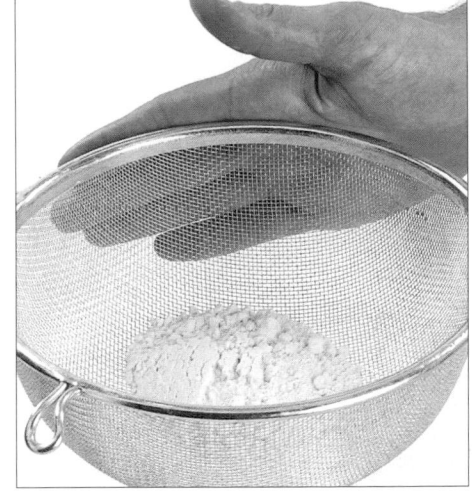

2 Season the flour with salt and pepper and sift it onto a sheet of parchment paper.

3 Lightly beat the eggs in the shallow dish. Mix the breadcrumbs and Parmesan cheese together in the small bowl and spread on another sheet of parchment paper.

4 Lay each veal slice in the seasoned flour to coat, then turn and coat the other side.

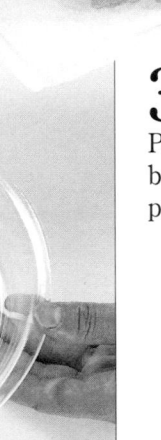

Breadcrumb and cheese mixture adheres easily to egg-coated veal

6 Finally, press each veal slice into the breadcrumb and cheese mixture and coat both sides evenly. Put each coated veal slice on a plate or another sheet of paper. Chill the scaloppine, uncovered, in the refrigerator while you sauté the bell peppers.

ANNE SAYS
"Coating will dry and be extra crisp if scaloppine are chilled 1–4 hours before frying."

5 Using 2 forks, dip each floured veal slice in the beaten egg and coat it thoroughly on both sides.

2 SAUTE THE BELL PEPPERS

1 Set the flat side of the chef's knife on top of the garlic clove and strike it with your fist. Discard the skin and finely chop the garlic. Strip the oregano leaves from the stems, reserving 6 of the top sprigs for garnish. Finely chop the leaves with the chef's knife.

2 With the small knife, cut around the core of each bell pepper and pull it out. Halve each pepper lengthwise and scrape out the seeds. Cut away the white ribs on the inside.

3 Set each bell pepper half cut-side down on the work surface, flatten it with the heel of your hand, and slice it lengthwise into thin strips.

When bell pepper strips are sliced thinly they will soften quickly in hot oil

Add bell pepper strips to frying pan all at once

4 Heat the oil in a medium frying pan. Add the garlic, bell pepper strips, salt, and pepper, and cook, stirring occasionally, until softened, 7–10 minutes. Remove from the heat, add the chopped oregano, and taste for seasoning; keep warm while cooking the scaloppine.

3 MAKE THE GARNISH AND COOK THE VEAL

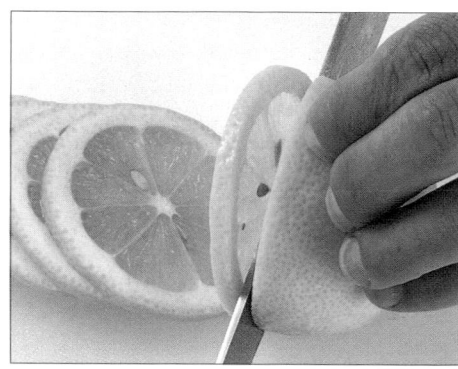

1 Slice the lemon for the garnish, and set aside. Heat half of the butter and 1 tbsp olive oil in a large frying pan.

2 Add 2–3 scaloppine to the pan and fry over medium-high heat until golden brown, 1–2 minutes.

ANNE SAYS
"The scaloppine should not touch or they will stick together."

Cook scaloppine in batches to avoid crowding in pan

If coating catches, wipe out pan and add more oil between batches

3 Turn the scaloppine with the 2-pronged fork, and continue cooking until brown on the outside and no longer pink in the center, about 1–2 minutes. Transfer to a plate lined with paper towels and keep warm. Add the remaining butter and oil to the pan and fry the remaining veal, adding more oil to the pan if necessary.

🍽 TO SERVE

Transfer the scaloppine to warmed individual plates and garnish each with a lemon slice and a sprig of oregano. Spoon bell pepper strips alongside.

Coating is crisp and golden brown

Bell pepper strips make bright color contrast

VARIATION

VEAL SCALOPPINE WITH PROSCIUTTO

Scaloppine topped with prosciutto and cheese are baked until the cheese melts to form Scaloppine alla Modenese.

1 Coat the veal scaloppine as directed in the main recipe, omitting the Parmesan cheese and using double the amount of breadcrumbs.

2 Grate 4 oz fontina or Gruyère cheese. Trim the fat from 6 thin slices of prosciutto (total weight of slices about $2^{1}/_{2}$ oz) so they are smaller than the veal scaloppine.

3 Omit the green bell pepper. Cut the red bell pepper into strips as directed in the main recipe. Peel 1 onion, leaving a little of the root attached, and cut lengthwise in half. Cut across into thin slices. Heat 2 tbsp olive oil in a frying pan, add the onion and sauté until soft, 2–3 minutes. Add the pepper strips and continue sautéing as directed in the main recipe.

4 Heat the oven to 400°F. Fry the scaloppine as directed.

5 Put the cooked scaloppine on a baking sheet. Lay a prosciutto slice on each veal slice and sprinkle with the grated cheese.

6 Bake the scaloppine in the heated oven until the cheese topping is melted and bubbling, 5–7 minutes.

7 Serve on warmed individual plates with wedges of lemon. If you like, garnish each scaloppine with a sprig of flat-leaf parsley.

SAUTEED LIVER AND ONIONS

Fegato alla Veneziana

🍴 SERVES 6 　🥣 WORK TIME 15–20 MINUTES 　🍲 COOKING TIME 35–40 MINUTES

EQUIPMENT

colander

large frying pan

chef's knife

metal spatula

small knife

slotted spoon

wooden spoon

bowl

aluminum foil

chopping board

potato masher †

saucepans, 1 with lid

pepper mill

† potato ricer can also be used

This delicious recipe for liver and onions is a classic Venetian dish, which is now found throughout Italy. Very thin slices of calf's liver are quickly sautéed in olive oil and served with meltingly soft caramelized onions and buttery mashed potatoes.

GETTING AHEAD

The onions can be sautéed up to 8 hours ahead and reheated; make sure you leave the oil in the frying pan. Prepare the mashed potatoes and sauté the liver just before serving.

SHOPPING LIST

2 lb	large onions
6 tbsp	olive oil
	salt and freshly ground black pepper
1¹/₂ lb	calf's liver
	For the mashed potatoes
1¹/₄ lb	potatoes
¹/₄ cup	milk
¹/₄ cup	butter

INGREDIENTS

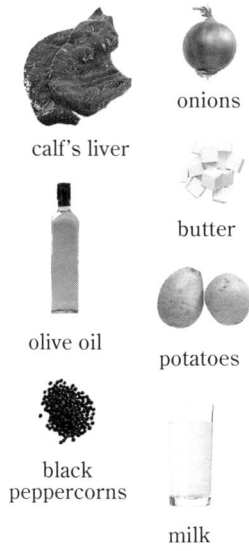

onions

calf's liver

butter

olive oil

potatoes

black peppercorns

milk

ANNE SAYS

"*Try to find calf's liver in one piece so that you can cut it into the thinnest possible slices yourself, rather than buying it pre-sliced by your butcher.*"

ORDER OF WORK

1 PREPARE THE ONIONS

2 PREPARE THE MASHED POTATOES

3 PREPARE THE LIVER

1 PREPARE THE ONIONS

1 Slice the onions (see box, below). Heat two-thirds of the oil in the frying pan. Add the onions with a little salt and pepper, and cover with foil.

2 Cook the onions over low heat, stirring occasionally, until very soft, 25–30 minutes. Meanwhile, prepare the mashed potatoes (see page 70).

Slow cooking develops sweetness of onions

Stir onions to prevent sticking

3 Remove the foil from the onions, increase the heat to medium-high, and cook, stirring constantly, until the onions are golden brown and caramelized, 5–7 minutes longer.

Stir onions so they caramelize evenly

! TAKE CARE !
Do not let the onions catch on the bottom of the pan or they will taste bitter.

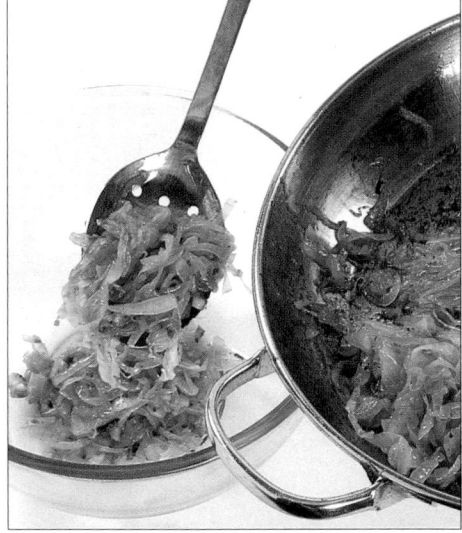

4 Transfer the onions to the bowl with the slotted spoon, leaving any excess oil in the pan to sauté the liver.

HOW TO SLICE AN ONION

Onions are often sliced for soups and stews, as well as for sautéing. The root is left on for slicing, to help hold the onion together.

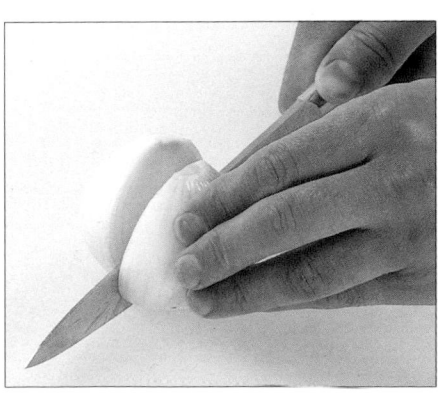

Use your knuckles to guide blade of knife

1 Peel the onion and trim the top, leaving a little of the root attached. Cut the onion lengthwise in half.

2 Put one half, cut-side down, on a chopping board. Holding the onion firmly, slice it crosswise, guiding the knife with bent fingers. Discard the root. Repeat with the other onion half.

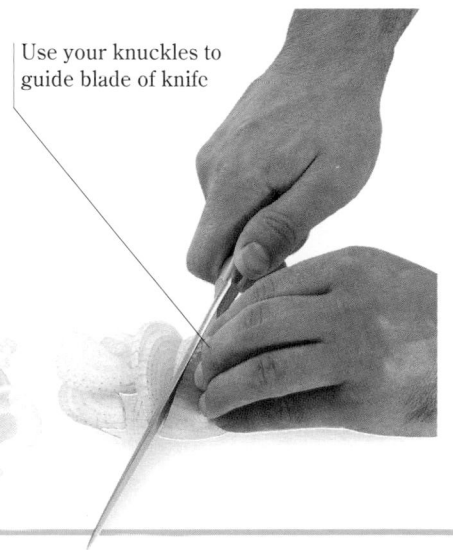

2 PREPARE THE MASHED POTATOES

1 Wash and peel the potatoes and cut them into pieces. Bring a medium saucepan of salted water to a boil. Add the potatoes, cover, and cook until tender when pierced with the small knife, 15–20 minutes.

2 Drain the potatoes thoroughly. Return them to the pan and mash with the potato masher. Heat the milk in a small saucepan. Add the butter, salt, and pepper, and beat until mixed. Gradually add the hot milk to the potatoes, beating constantly until the potatoes are light and fluffy, about 5 minutes. Taste for seasoning and keep warm.

Butter will melt into milk

3 PREPARE THE LIVER

1 With your fingers, peel any skin from the liver. Cut off any exposed ducts or connective tissue. Cut the liver into thin slices, about 1/4-inch thick. If more than 3 inches long, cut them in half.

Sharp chef's knife cuts liver cleanly and does not tear fibers

2 Remove any internal ducts, and season the liver with salt and freshly ground pepper.

ANNE SAYS
"Season the liver just before frying because salt draws out the juices."

Thin, uniform slices of meat will cook quickly and evenly

3 Add the remaining oil to the frying pan and heat the oil over high heat. Add half of the liver and cook just until browned, 45–60 seconds.

4 Turn the slices with the metal spatula and brown the other side, 45–60 seconds.

5 The slices should cook very quickly in a single layer without overlapping, so they are browned on the outside but still pink in the center.

ANNE SAYS
"Liver should always be pink in the center. Do not overcook it or it will be tough."

6 Transfer the liver to a plate and keep warm. Cook the remaining liver in the same way.

7 Return the onions to the pan with all of the liver and stir quickly over high heat until very hot, 30–60 seconds. Season with salt and pepper.

Liver and onions are reheated quickly together

🍽 TO SERVE
Reheat the mashed potatoes if necessary. Transfer liver and onions to warmed individual plates, and serve at once, with the potatoes.

Creamy mashed potatoes are classic accompaniment

Caramelized onions are key ingredient

SAUTEED LIVER WITH WINE VINEGAR

Fegato all'Aceto is a tangy variation of Sautéed Liver and Onions.

1 Omit the onions. Strip the leaves from 1 medium bunch of flat-leaf or curly parsley and pile them on a chopping board. Finely chop the leaves, using a chef's knife. Cut the liver into thin slices as directed in the main recipe.

2 Heat 2 tbsp oil and 2 tbsp butter in a large frying pan over high heat. Add half of the liver and cook as directed until browned on both sides but still slightly pink in the center.

3 Cook the remaining liver in the same way, keeping the first batch warm.

4 Reduce the heat to medium, return the first batch of liver to the pan, and pour over 1/4 cup red wine vinegar. Sprinkle with the parsley, season with salt and pepper, and stir to mix.

5 Serve on warmed individual plates, accompanied by slices of fried polenta, if you like.

DEVILED CHICKEN

Pollo alla Diavola

EQUIPMENT

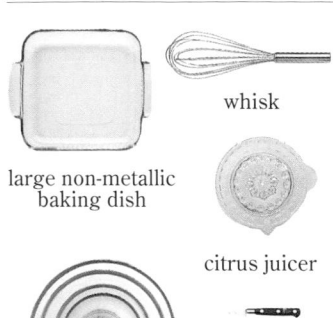

large non-metallic baking dish

whisk

citrus juicer

small knife

bowls

paper towels

chef's knife

2-pronged fork

pepper mill

poultry shears

pastry brush   rubber gloves

2 long metal skewers

chopping board

ANNE SAYS
"*Deviled chicken is very suited to grilling on the barbecue. In this case, bake the tomatoes separately in a baking dish. Spoon the crumb-herb mixture on them, then bake in a 400°F oven, 10–12 minutes.*"

An abundance of chili pepper gives this hot chicken dish its name. The backbone is removed from the chicken, which is then flattened and marinated in lemon juice, chili pepper, and black pepper. Tomatoes topped with garlic, parsley, and olive oil are broiled with the chicken to serve as an accompaniment.

GETTING AHEAD
The chicken can be marinated up to 1 day ahead – it will be spicier. Broil it with the tomatoes just before serving.

*plus 8 hours marinating time

SHOPPING LIST

1	small chicken, weighing about 3 lb
4	lemons
2	fresh hot red chili peppers
2 tbsp	olive oil, more for broiler rack
	salt and freshly ground black pepper
	For the broiled tomatoes
2	large tomatoes, total weight about 1 lb
5–7	sprigs of flat-leaf parsley
2	garlic cloves
1/4 cup	dry breadcrumbs
1 tbsp	olive oil

INGREDIENTS

chicken

lemons

fresh hot red chili peppers †

tomatoes

garlic cloves

flat-leaf parsley ‡

dry breadcrumbs

black peppercorns

olive oil

† dried hot red chili peppers can also be used

‡ curly parsley can also be used

ORDER OF WORK

1 SPLIT AND FLATTEN THE CHICKEN

2 MARINATE THE CHICKEN

3 PREPARE THE TOMATOES

4 BROIL THE CHICKEN AND TOMATOES

1 SPLIT AND FLATTEN THE CHICKEN

1 Set the chicken breast-side down on the chopping board. With the poultry shears, cut along each side of the backbone.

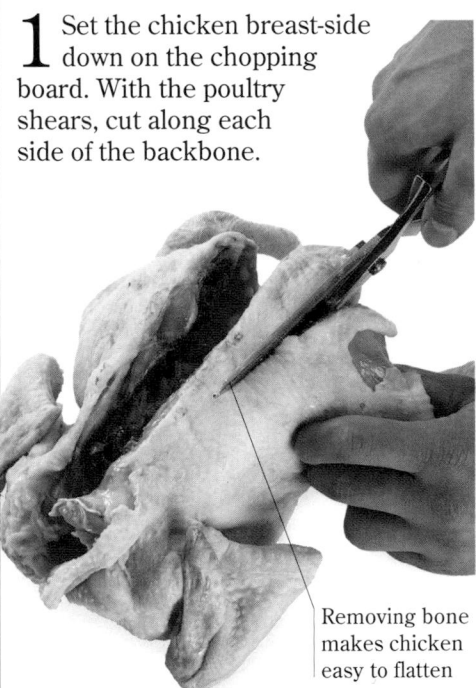

Removing bone makes chicken easy to flatten

2 Discard the backbone from the chicken and, using the chef's knife, trim off any flaps of skin.

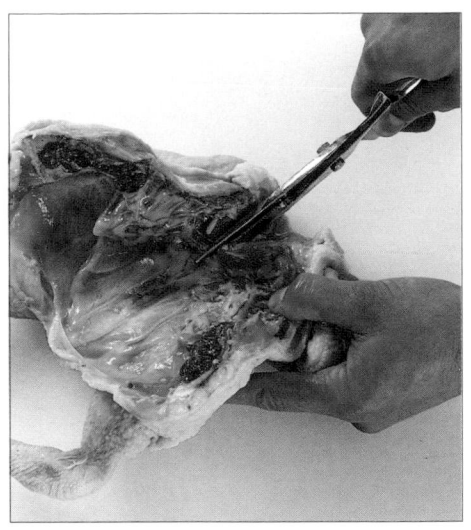

3 Force the bird open and, with the poultry shears, snip the wishbone. Wipe the bird inside and outside with paper towels.

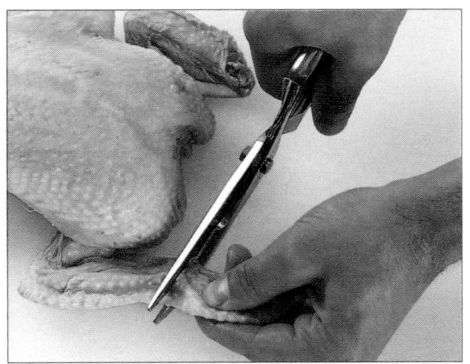

4 Turn the bird breast-side up, cut off the wing tips, and discard them. Turn the legs inward.

Use both hands to break breastbone of chicken

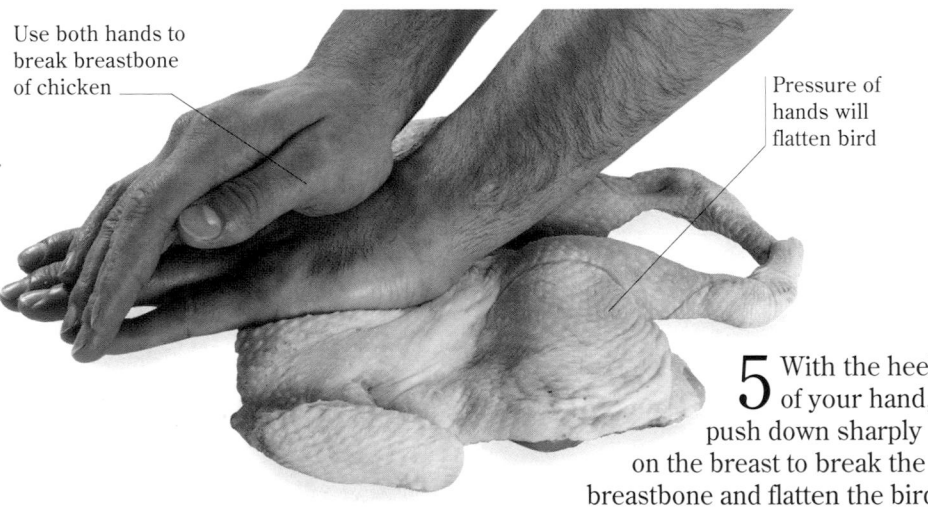

Pressure of hands will flatten bird

5 With the heel of your hand, push down sharply on the breast to break the breastbone and flatten the bird.

Chicken legs are secured by tucking into slits in skin

6 Using the small knife, make a small cut in the skin between the leg and breastbone and tuck in the end of the leg.

7 Holding the legs carefully in position, set the flattened chicken in the large baking dish.

2 MARINATE THE CHICKEN

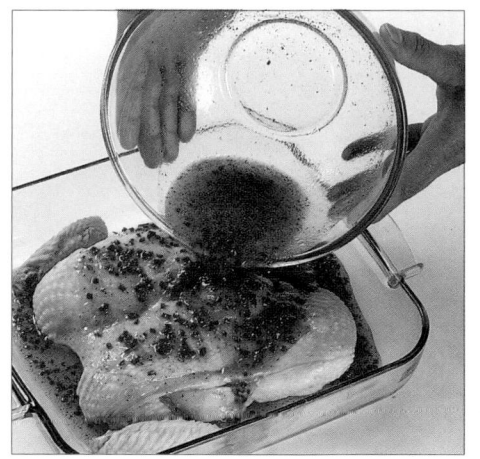

1 Squeeze the juice from 3 of the lemons – there should be about ½ cup juice. If using fresh chili peppers, core, seed, and dice them (see box, below). If using dried chilis, chop them.

2 Whisk the lemon juice, diced chili peppers, oil, and 2 tsp freshly ground black pepper in a bowl until thoroughly mixed.

3 Pour the marinade over the chicken. Cover and leave to marinate in the refrigerator 8 hours, turning and basting the chicken occasionally.

HOW TO CORE, SEED, AND DICE FRESH HOT CHILI PEPPERS

Fresh hot chili peppers must be finely chopped so their heat is spread evenly through the dish. For a hotter flavor, you can add the seeds too. Chili peppers can burn your skin, so be sure to wear rubber gloves, and to avoid contact with eyes.

Remove all seeds unless very hot flavor is wanted

1 Cut the chili peppers lengthwise in half with a small knife. Cut out the core and fleshy white ribs and scrape out the seeds.

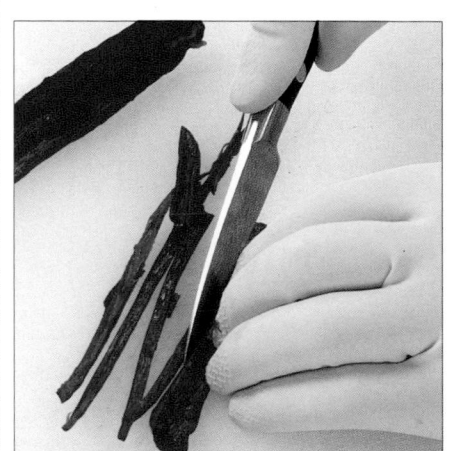

2 Set each chili pepper half cut-side up and thinly slice it lengthwise into strips with the small knife.

3 Gather the chili pepper strips together with your fingers and cut them across to produce very fine dice.

3 PREPARE THE TOMATOES

Tomato halves are ready for crumb-herb topping

1 Cut the cores from the tomatoes. Cut the tomatoes horizontally in half with the chef's knife.

2 If necessary, cut a small slice off the base of each half so it will sit flat on the broiler rack; set aside.

Pull leaves gently from stems

Flecks of parsley will add color as well as flavor to baked tomatoes

3 Strip the parsley leaves from the stems, reserving a few sprigs for decoration. Pile the leaves on the chopping board. With the chef's knife, finely chop them.

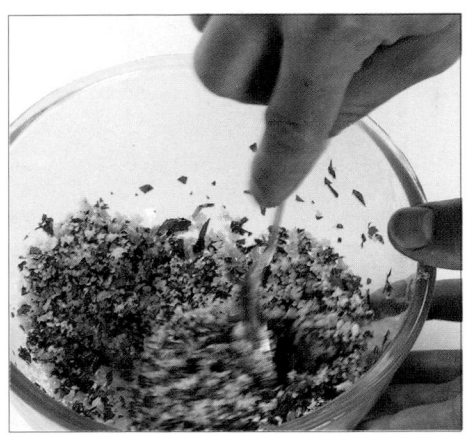

4 Set the flat side of the chef's knife on top of each garlic clove and strike it with your fist. Discard the skins and finely chop the garlic.

5 Put the chopped parsley, garlic, breadcrumbs, and oil into a small bowl, and season generously with salt and freshly ground black pepper.

6 Stir the crumb-herb mixture thoroughly until well mixed together; set aside.

4 BROIL THE CHICKEN AND TOMATOES

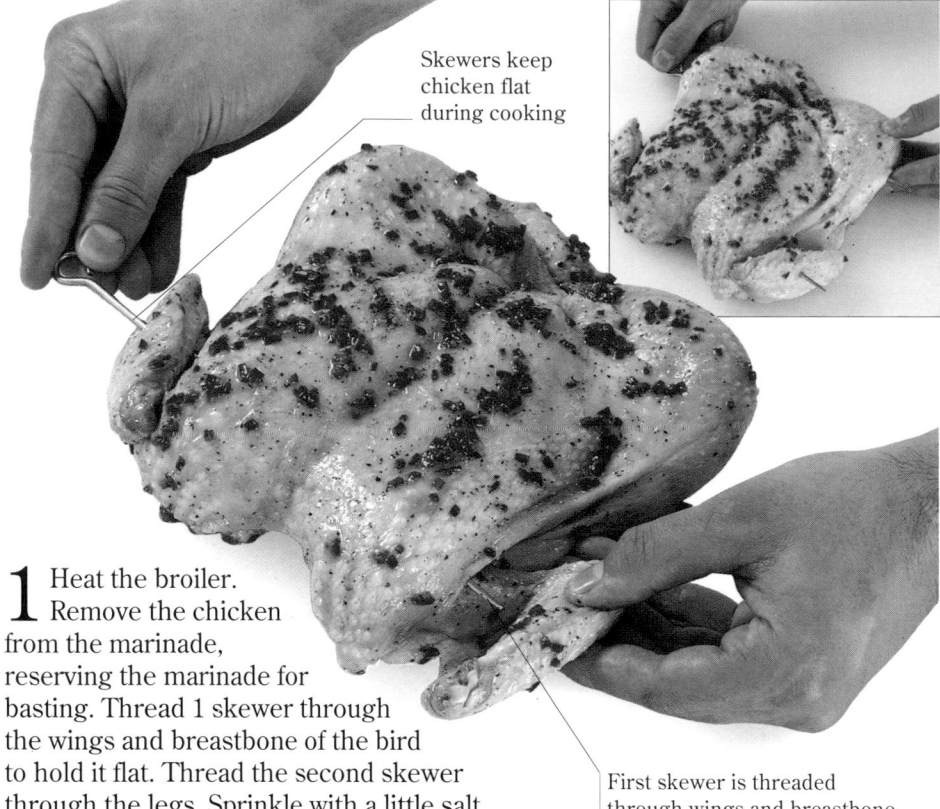

Skewers keep chicken flat during cooking

First skewer is threaded through wings and breastbone

1 Heat the broiler. Remove the chicken from the marinade, reserving the marinade for basting. Thread 1 skewer through the wings and breastbone of the bird to hold it flat. Thread the second skewer through the legs. Sprinkle with a little salt.

2 Brush the broiler rack with oil and set the chicken on it, skin-side up. Broil the chicken about 4 inches from the heat, basting occasionally with the reserved marinade, until the skin is golden brown, 15–20 minutes.

3 Remove the broiler pan from the heat and turn over the chicken. Set the 4 tomato halves alongside, cut-side up. Continue broiling, basting the chicken from time to time, 10–15 minutes longer.

Crumb-herb topping turns golden brown when broiled

4 Turn the chicken again and spoon the crumb-herb mixture onto the tomatoes. Continue cooking, basting the chicken often, until the skin is slightly charred. The juices from the thigh should run clear when the meat is pierced, 10–15 minutes longer. The tomatoes should be tender and browned on top; if necessary, broil them a few minutes longer.

ANNE SAYS
"If the skin of the chicken browns too quickly during broiling, turn the chicken over again and cook so the skin side is away from the heat."

5 While the chicken is cooking, cut the remaining lemon into slices; reserve the slices for decoration.

Cut chicken across so some white meat is included with leg

6 Remove the skewers from the chicken. Holding the chicken with the 2-pronged fork, split the breastbone with the chef's knife, dividing the bird in half. Cut each half across to make 4 even portions.

🍴 **TO SERVE**

Transfer the chicken pieces and tomato halves to warmed plates. Decorate with the reserved lemon and parsley.

Crisp chicken skin is flecked with pieces of chili pepper

Juicy broiled tomatoes are a foil to piquant chicken

VARIATION

BROILED CHICKEN DRUMSTICKS WITH ROSEMARY

Gambe di Pollo ai Ferri make delicious picnic fare. You can cook chicken wings or whole legs in the same way.

1 Substitute 8 chicken drumsticks for the whole chicken and make a garlic-herb marinade in place of the deviled mixture: peel and finely chop 3 garlic cloves. Remove the leaves from 8–10 sprigs of fresh rosemary and finely chop the leaves.

2 Mix the garlic and rosemary with the juice of 1 lemon, ⅓ cup olive oil, and black pepper to taste. Marinate the chicken as directed.

3 Remove the drumsticks from the marinade. Sprinkle them with salt, and broil or grill them, turning and basting occasionally, until the juices run clear when the chicken is pierced with a fork, 20–30 minutes.

4 Omit the baked tomatoes. Arrange the drumsticks on a serving platter and surround with sliced tomatoes sprinkled with a little olive oil, lemon juice, and finely chopped fresh parsley.

SPINACH-STUFFED VEAL ROLLS

Messicani di Vitello

🍽️ SERVES 4 🥣 WORK TIME 45–50 MINUTES ☕ COOKING TIME 30–40 MINUTES

EQUIPMENT

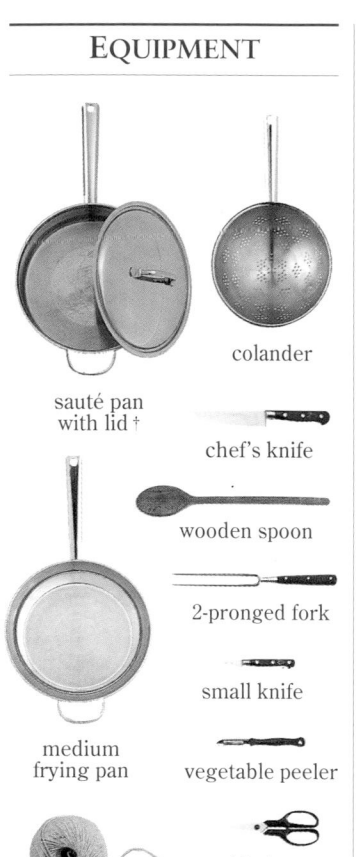

colander

sauté pan with lid †

chef's knife

wooden spoon

2-pronged fork

small knife

medium frying pan

vegetable peeler

kitchen string

kitchen scissors

nutmeg grater

strainer

saucepans

rolling pin

parchment paper ‡

† shallow casserole can also be used

‡ wax paper or plastic wrap can also be used

Thin slices of veal are rolled around a stuffing of spinach, Parmesan, and walnuts. Scaloppine of all sorts are popular in Italy. Beef, pork, chicken, and turkey are all possibilities, but the national favorite is still veal.

GETTING AHEAD

The veal rolls can be cooked up to 2 days ahead and refrigerated, or they can be frozen. Their flavor mellows on standing. Reheat them, in the sauce, on top of the stove.

SHOPPING LIST

8	veal scaloppine, total weight about 1¼ lb
1	medium onion
1	carrot
2	celery stalks
2 tbsp	olive oil, more if needed
1 cup	dry white wine
1 cup	chicken stock (see box, page 123), more if needed
	For the stuffing
8	garlic cloves
⅓ cup	walnuts
1 lb	fresh or 10 oz defrosted spinach
2 tbsp	olive oil
¼ cup	freshly grated Parmesan cheese
	salt and pepper
	freshly grated nutmeg

INGREDIENTS

veal scaloppine

grated Parmesan cheese

spinach

nutmeg †

walnuts

garlic cloves

dry white wine

chicken stock ‡

olive oil

onion

celery

carrot

† ground nutmeg can also be used

‡ water can also be used

ANNE SAYS
"Potatoes roasted with olive oil and herbs would make an excellent accompaniment."

ORDER OF WORK

1 PREPARE THE STUFFING; ROLL THE SCALOPPINE

2 PREPARE THE VEGETABLES; COOK THE VEAL ROLLS

1 PREPARE THE STUFFING; ROLL THE SCALOPPINE

1 Set the flat side of the chef's knife on top of each garlic clove and strike it with your fist. Discard the skins and finely chop the garlic. Coarsely chop the walnuts.

2 If using fresh spinach, wash, cook, and drain the leaves (see box, below). Squeeze defrosted spinach to remove excess water. Using the chef's knife, chop the spinach.

3 Heat the oil in the frying pan and add the spinach. Cook, stirring, until any moisture has evaporated, 2–3 minutes. Remove from the heat and add half of the garlic, the walnuts, Parmesan cheese, salt and pepper, and freshly grated nutmeg. Stir the stuffing ingredients well to combine, and taste for seasoning.

HOW TO PREPARE AND COOK SPINACH

The tough stems and ribs must be removed from fresh spinach so the leaves will not be stringy after they are cooked. Thorough draining of all moisture after cooking is essential.

1 Tear the tough stems and ribs from the spinach leaves with your hands. Wash the leaves thoroughly in plenty of cold water.

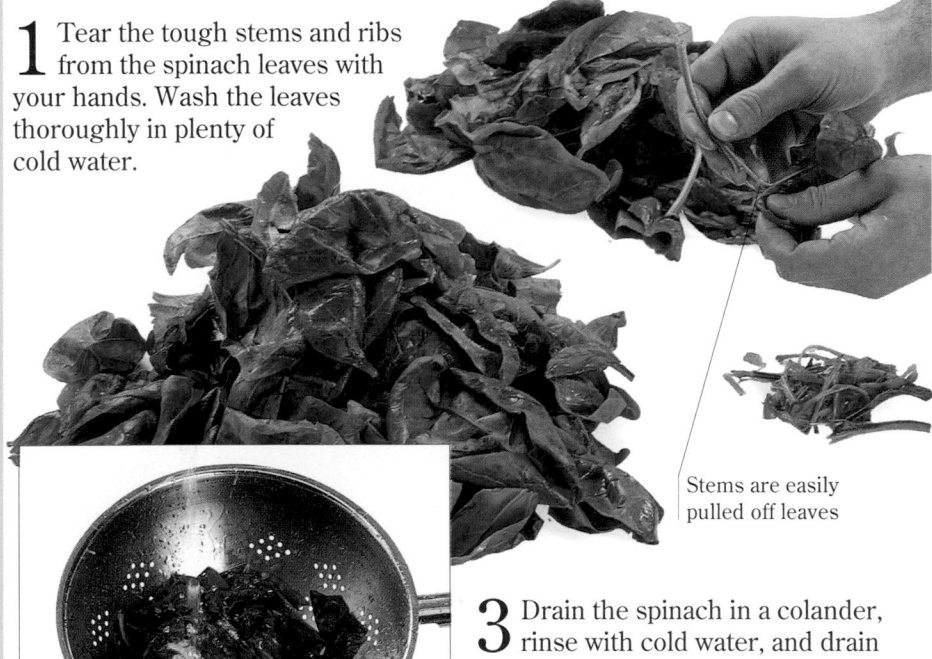

Stems are easily pulled off leaves

2 Bring a large saucepan of salted water to boiling, add the spinach and simmer until tender, 1–2 minutes.

3 Drain the spinach in a colander, rinse with cold water, and drain again thoroughly.

4 When cool, squeeze the spinach in your fist to remove excess water.

4 If necessary, flatten the scaloppine: put 2 veal slices between 2 sheets of parchment paper. Pound to 1/8-inch thickness with the rolling pin. Repeat with the remaining scaloppine.

! TAKE CARE !
Flatten veal gently so holes do not form in the meat.

Pounding veal tenderizes flesh

5 Lay 1 veal scaloppine on the work surface and sprinkle with salt and pepper. Spread about one-eighth of the spinach stuffing on top.

6 Roll up the meat, tucking in the ends. Repeat with the remaining scaloppine and spinach stuffing.

7 Tie up the 8 rolls in neat packages. Alternatively, you can secure each roll with a wooden toothpick, threading it in and out along the seam, and catching in the ends.

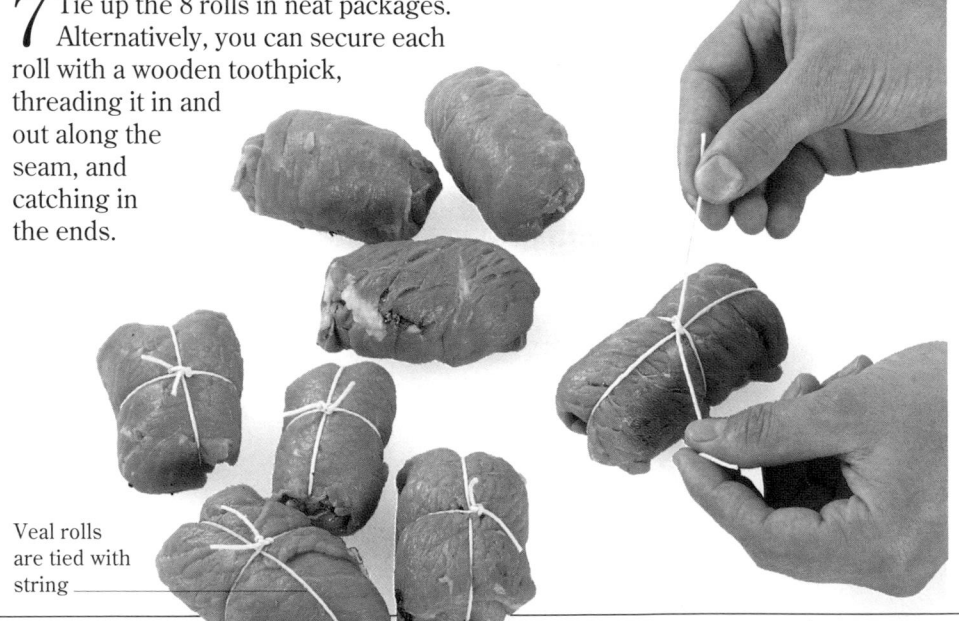

Veal rolls are tied with string

PREPARE THE VEGETABLES; COOK THE VEAL ROLLS

1 Peel the onion, leaving a little of the root attached, and cut it lengthwise in half through the root and stem. Lay each onion half flat on the chopping board and, with the chef's knife, cut it across into thin slices.

Slice all vegetables the same size to cook evenly

2 Peel and trim the carrot. Cut it lengthwise into quarters and then across into thin slices. Thinly slice the celery stalks, with the chef's knife.

3 Heat 2 tbsp olive oil in the sauté pan and add the veal rolls. Cook them over high heat, turning occasionally, until they are well browned on all sides, 2–3 minutes. Transfer the rolls to a plate, using the 2-pronged fork, and set them aside.

4 If necessary, add 1–2 tbsp more oil to the sauté pan. Add the onion with the remaining garlic and cook, stirring, until softened, 2–3 minutes. Stir in the carrot and celery. Lower the heat and cook, stirring occasionally, until tender, 8–10 minutes. Pour in the wine, bring to a boil, and simmer until reduced by half, 3–5 minutes.

5 Return the veal rolls with any juices to the sauté pan and add the stock with salt and pepper to taste. Cover the pan and simmer, stirring occasionally, until the veal is very tender, 30–40 minutes.

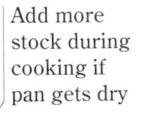

Add more stock during cooking if pan gets dry

Well-browned veal rolls are cooked on bed of vegetables

6 Return the veal rolls to the plate. Strain the cooking liquid into a saucepan, reserving the vegetables. If necessary, boil the liquid until it is reduced to ³/₄ cup; taste for seasoning.

Reserve vegetables for serving with veal rolls

Vegetables cooked with veal rolls are full of flavor

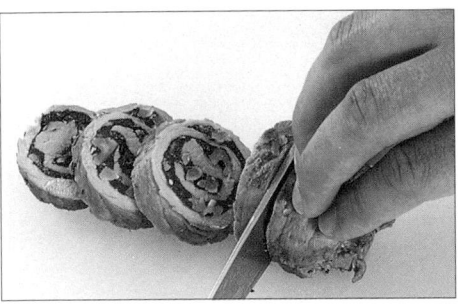

7 Meanwhile, discarding the string or toothpicks, cut the veal rolls across into slices about ³/₈-inch thick. Arrange on warmed individual plates with the vegetables piled in the center. Spoon on the cooking liquid and serve.

Filling is colorful and crunchy

ROAST PORK LOIN WITH GARLIC AND ROSEMARY

Arista

†●︎❙ SERVES 6–8 🥣 **WORK TIME 15–20 MINUTES** 🍲 **ROASTING TIME 1–1½ HOURS**

EQUIPMENT

food processor †

medium roasting pan

bowl

rubber spatula

chef's knife   pastry brush

metal skewer

aluminum foil

2-pronged fork

large metal spoon

kitchen string

chopping board

† blender or mortar and pestle can also be used

The Italian name for this boneless pork loin, oven-roasted with a pungent stuffing and coating of garlic, fresh rosemary, and black peppercorns, is taken from the Greek and translates as "the best". What more can I say? Zucchini or yellow squash slices sautéed in olive oil with finely chopped shallots make a simple and colorful accompaniment.

GETTING AHEAD
The pork loin can be roasted up to 1 day ahead and refrigerated, tightly wrapped in foil. It is delicious served cold.

SHOPPING LIST

10	garlic cloves
1	small bunch of fresh rosemary
2 tsp	black peppercorns
	salt
2 tbsp	olive oil, more for roasting pan
3 lb	boneless pork loin
1 cup	water, more if needed

INGREDIENTS

boneless pork loin

olive oil

fresh rosemary

garlic cloves

peppercorns

ANNE SAYS
"After the butcher has removed the rib bones from the pork loin, what is left is the eye of meat with a flap of meat attached."

ORDER OF WORK

1 MAKE THE GARLIC AND ROSEMARY STUFFING

2 PREPARE AND STUFF THE PORK LOIN

1 MAKE THE GARLIC AND ROSEMARY STUFFING

1 Set the flat side of the chef's knife on top of each garlic clove and strike it with your fist. Discard the skins and put the garlic in the bowl of the food processor.

Crushing garlic cloves loosens skin for easy peeling

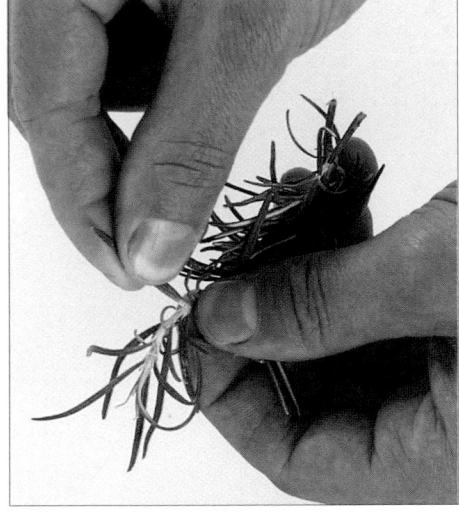

2 Strip the rosemary leaves from the stems and add them to the garlic with the peppercorns and salt.

3 Work the ingredients in the food processor, using the pulse button, until finely chopped.

ANNE SAYS
"*Keep the mixture coarse if you like pieces of cracked pepper.*"

2 PREPARE AND STUFF THE PORK LOIN

1 Heat the oven to 400°F. Using the pastry brush, lightly brush the roasting pan with olive oil.

2 Cut away and discard any excess fat and sinew from the pork loin, using the chef's knife.

Stuffing is enclosed by natural flap of pork loin

3 Fold open the flap of meat and, using the rubber spatula, spread half of the garlic and rosemary stuffing over the meat. Fold the flap of meat back over the garlic and herb mixture and reshape the loin.

ANNE SAYS
"*If your pork loin does not have a separate flap of meat, make a deep horizontal slit through the meat with the chef's knife, almost to the other side.*"

4 Using separate pieces of string, tie the roll of pork at 1-inch intervals to hold its shape during cooking.

String keeps pork loin in shape during roasting

String should be tied tightly because pork loin shrinks during cooking

5 Set the pork in the prepared roasting pan and spread the remaining stuffing over the outside of the pork. Sprinkle with the olive oil.

6 Roast the pork in the oven until it starts to brown, 20–25 minutes. Remove from the oven and pour half of the water over the pork.

7 Using the 2-pronged fork, turn the meat over. Continue roasting the pork 45–60 minutes longer, turning it 2 or 3 times during cooking so it browns evenly, adding half of the remaining water when the pan becomes dry.

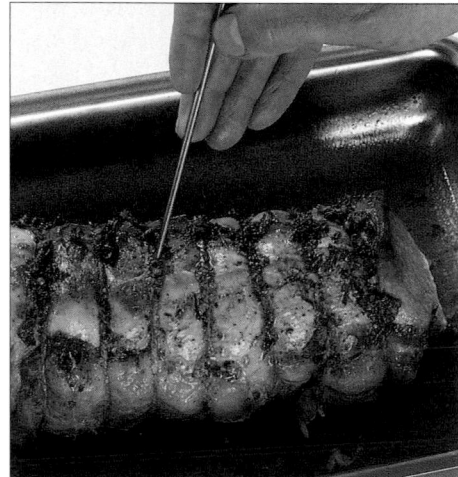

8 The pork is cooked when the skewer inserted in the center of the loin 30 seconds is very hot to the touch when withdrawn.

9 Transfer the meat to the chopping board, cover it with foil, and let stand for 10 minutes to allow the juices to be reabsorbed before carving.

Foil keeps meat warm while finishing dish

10 Using the large metal spoon, discard some of the fat from the roasting pan. Add the remaining water and boil, stirring, to dissolve the pan juices. Taste for seasoning.

11 Remove and discard the strings from the pork loin and cut the pork into slices about ³/₈-inch thick.

Sharp chef's knife helps in cutting slices of even thickness

Hold loin steady with 2-pronged fork

Lively mixture of garlic, rosemary, and pepper stuffs and tops the meat

🍽 TO SERVE

Arrange the pork slices on a warmed serving dish, with zucchini slices, if you like, and spoon over the pan juices.

Zucchini slices, sautéed in olive oil with chopped shallots, are delicious with pork

VARIATION

BRAISED PORK WITH MADEIRA SAUCE

In Arrosto di Maiale in Casseruola, *the pork loin is braised with onions.*

1 Heat the oven to 350°F. Make the stuffing with 5 garlic cloves, 3–5 sprigs of fresh rosemary, and 1 tsp black peppercorns. Peel and slice 2 onions.
2 Trim, stuff, and tie up the pork as directed, and season the outside.
3 Heat 3 tbsp olive oil in a casserole. Add the pork and brown on all sides over high heat, about 5 minutes, then remove. Add the onions with 2 bay leaves and cook over medium heat until slightly softened, 3–5 minutes.
4 Return the pork to the pan and pour in 1 cup water. Cover and cook in the oven until tender when pierced with a fork, 1³/₄–2 hours. Turn the pork 2–3 times during cooking and add more water if the onions seem dry.
5 Remove the pork and let stand.
6 Mix 1 tbsp Madeira wine and 1 tsp cornstarch to a paste. Spoon off any fat from the cooking liquid. Add 1 cup water, bring to a boil, and cook until reduced by half, stirring, 2–3 minutes. Strain into a small pan and heat to boiling. Add 3 tbsp Madeira and bring back to a boil. Whisk in the cornstarch paste until thickened. Taste for seasoning. Slice the pork loin, discarding the strings. Serve the pork with the sauce, and carrot batons, if you like.

Hunter's Chicken

Pollo alla Cacciatora

🍽 SERVES 4　🥄 WORK TIME 20–25 MINUTES　🍲 COOKING TIME 45–60 MINUTES

EQUIPMENT

slotted spoon

chef's knife

small knife

large sauté pan with lid

wooden spoon

pepper mill

large frying pan with lid

2-pronged fork

chopping board

Alla cacciatora *means hunter's style – the Italian way of cooking a bird after a shoot. Add your favorite herb, instead of rosemary, to the sauce – I find that sage works particularly well. The sautéed escarole shown here makes a flavorsome accompaniment.*

GETTING AHEAD

The chicken can be cooked up to 2 days ahead and refrigerated in the sauce. Reheat it on top of the stove, adding a little more stock if the sauce seems dry. Prepare the escarole just before serving.

SHOPPING LIST

3–3 1/2 lb	chicken, cut into 8 pieces
	salt and freshly ground black pepper
1/4 cup	olive oil
1	medium onion
4	garlic cloves
1	sprig of fresh rosemary
1	bay leaf
1/4 cup	dry white wine
1/2 cup	chicken stock (see box, page 123), more if needed
1	medium head of escarole, weighing about 1 1/2 lb
1/4 cup	water, more if needed

INGREDIENTS

chicken pieces　　olive oil

escarole　　fresh rosemary

garlic cloves

chicken stock †

bay leaf

dry white wine

peppercorns

onion

† water can also be used

ANNE SAYS

"*Two heads of radicchio, total weight about 12–14 oz, can be substituted for the escarole. Prepare them in the same way, cutting each head into 4 pieces.*"

ORDER OF WORK

1 SAUTE THE CHICKEN

2 SAUTE THE ESCAROLE

1 SAUTE THE CHICKEN

1 Season the chicken pieces all over with salt and freshly ground black pepper to taste.

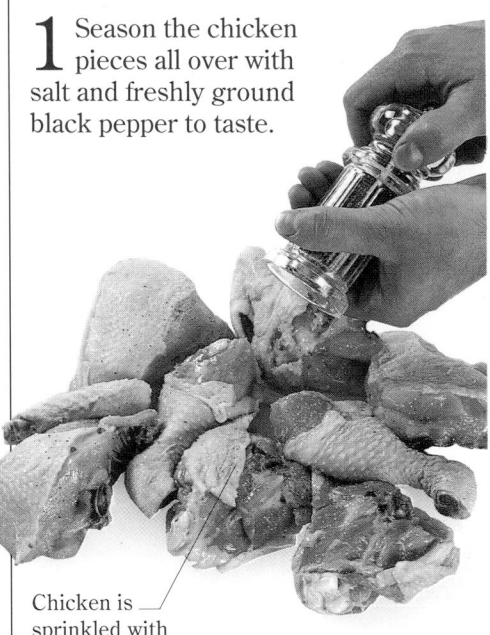

Chicken is sprinkled with black pepper

2 Heat half of the oil in the sauté pan over medium heat. Add the chicken thighs and drumsticks, skin-side down, and sauté until they begin to brown, about 5 minutes.

3 Add the chicken breast pieces, and continue cooking gently until very brown, 10–15 minutes. Turn and brown the other side.

4 Meanwhile, peel the onion, leaving a little of the root attached, and cut lengthwise in half.

5 Slice each of the onion halves horizontally toward the root, leaving the slices attached at the root end, and then slice vertically, again leaving the root end uncut. Finally, cut across the onion to make dice.

6 Set the flat side of the chef's knife on top of each garlic clove and strike it with your fist. Discard the skins and finely chop the garlic.

Skin of chicken is browned and crispy

Move chicken pieces to side of pan to make space in center

7 Add the chopped onion and half of the chopped garlic to the chicken, letting them fall to the bottom of the pan. Continue cooking gently until they are soft and golden brown, about 10 minutes.

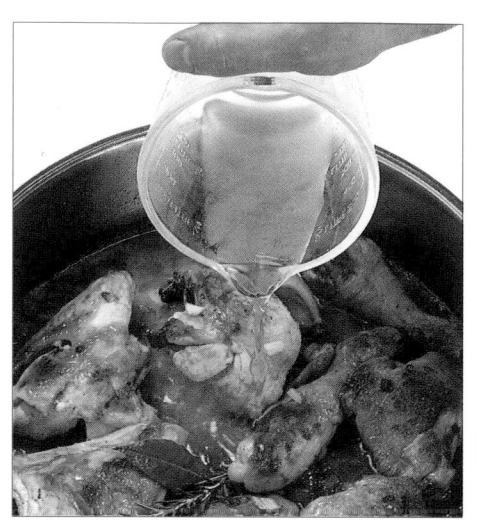

8 Add the sprig of rosemary, bay leaf, wine, chicken stock, salt, and pepper, and stir to mix.

At end of cooking, sauce is dark and reduced

9 Cover and simmer until the chicken is tender when pierced with the 2-pronged fork, 15–20 minutes. If the pan becomes dry during cooking, add a little more chicken stock. If some pieces of chicken cook before others, remove them from the pan and keep them warm. While the chicken is cooking, sauté the escarole.

2 SAUTE THE ESCAROLE

1 With the small knife, trim off the root end of the escarole. Discard any tough, green outer leaves, then wash well.

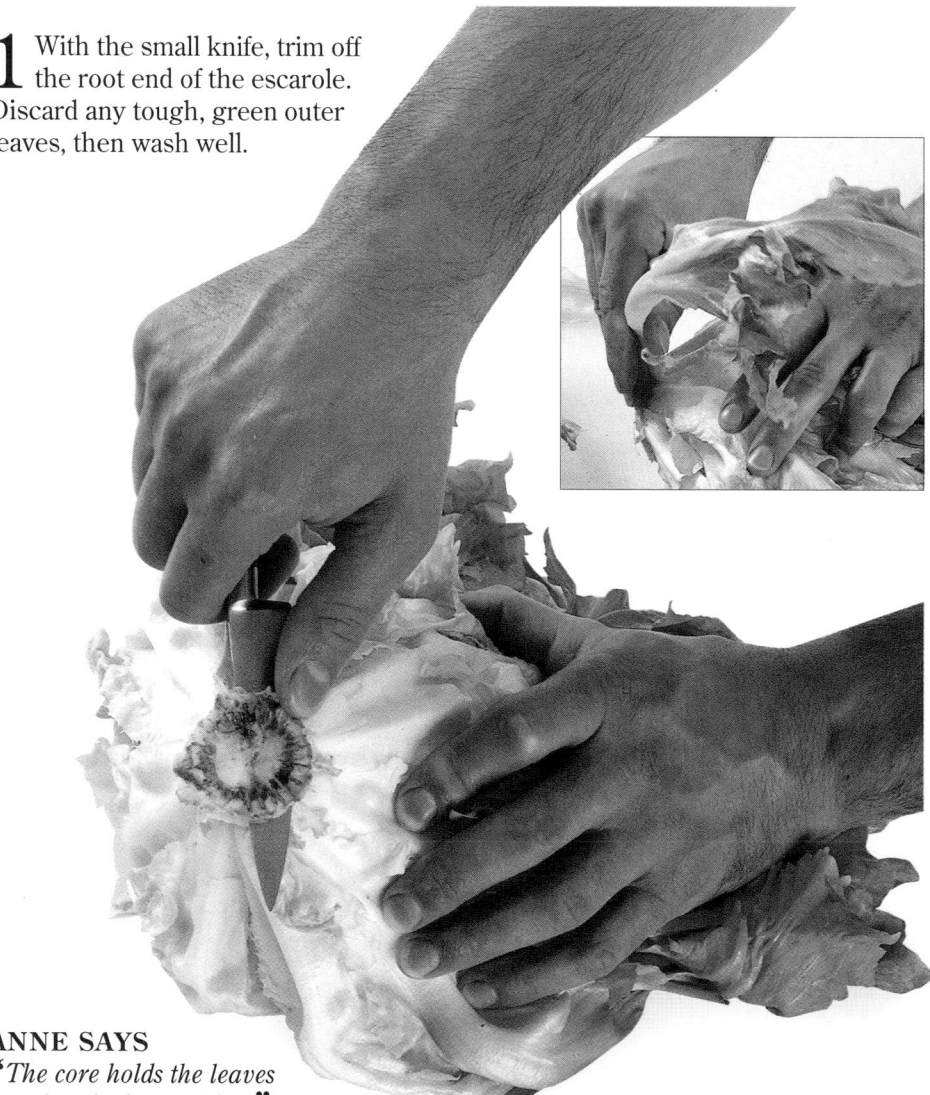

ANNE SAYS
"The core holds the leaves together during cooking."

2 Using the chef's knife, cut the escarole into 8 wedges, cutting through the core.

3 Heat the remaining oil in the frying pan. Add the rest of the garlic with the escarole, water, salt, and pepper. Bring to a boil, then cover and simmer gently, 10–20 minutes, depending on the toughness of the vegetable. Turn the escarole occasionally.

4 Test that the escarole is tender by piercing near the core with a knife. The liquid should have evaporated so the leaves are lightly glazed with oil.

! TAKE CARE !
If the escarole produces a great deal of liquid, remove the lid for the last 5–10 minutes of cooking so it can evaporate.

Sauce is thickened and reduced when chicken is cooked

5 Remove the chicken pieces from the pan and arrange on warmed individual plates. Discard the bay leaf and rosemary from the sauce, and taste for seasoning.

🍴 TO SERVE
Arrange the escarole next to the chicken, tucking large leaves under small ones to make neat packages. Spoon the sauce over the chicken, and serve with crusty bread, if you like.

Chicken is meltingly tender and full of flavor

Sautéed escarole is lightly glazed with olive oil and flavored with garlic

HUNTER'S CHICKEN WITH BLACK OLIVES

Pollo alla Cacciatora con le Olive *is a real treat for olive lovers. It is served here with sautéed Belgian endive.*

1 Omit the onion, chicken stock, rosemary, and bay leaf from the main recipe. Chop 5 garlic cloves.
2 Pit 1 cup Gaeta or oil-cured black olives, using an olive pitter. Chop half of the olives, leaving the rest whole. Chop 2 anchovy fillets.
3 Heat half of the oil in a large sauté pan and add half of the chopped garlic. Add the seasoned chicken pieces as directed, and sauté until all pieces are browned, 10–15 minutes.
4 Add the wine, 2 tbsp red wine vinegar, the chopped and whole olives, and the anchovies to the chicken. Cover and simmer the chicken as directed, adding a little water if the pan becomes dry.
5 Meanwhile, trim 2 medium heads of Belgian endive, total weight about 1/2 lb. Wipe them with a damp paper towel and discard any wilted leaves. Cut each head lengthwise into quarters, cutting through the core.
6 Cook the endive as for the escarole, until lightly browned.
7 Serve the chicken and endive on warmed plates. Spoon the olive sauce over the chicken.

STRAWBERRY AND RASPBERRY HAZELNUT TART

Crostata di Fragole e Lamponi

 SERVES 6–8   WORK TIME 35–40 MINUTES*   BAKING TIME 30–35 MINUTES

EQUIPMENT

food processor †

9- to 10-inch tart pan, with removable base

bowls

pastry bag and medium star tube

baking sheet

small knife

pastry brush

chef's knife

whisk ‡

strainer

rubber spatula

metal spatula

wooden spoon

chopping board

pastry scraper

† blender can also be used
‡ electric mixer can also be used

INGREDIENTS

strawberries

confectioners' sugar

granulated sugar

hazelnuts

raspberries

flour

unsalted butter

heavy cream

Marsala wine

egg

Traditionally, Italian fruit tarts are simple – often nothing more than fresh fruit on a pastry crust. Here, red berries top hazelnut pastry, decked with Marsala-accented whipped cream.

GETTING AHEAD

The dough can be made up to 2 days ahead and refrigerated, or it can be frozen. You can bake the hazelnut pastry round 6–8 hours ahead. Assemble the tart not more than 2 hours before serving.

*plus 45 minutes chilling time

SHOPPING LIST

1 cup	heavy cream
3–4 tbsp	confectioners' sugar
2 tbsp	Marsala wine
1 pint	strawberries
3/4 cup	raspberries
	For the hazelnut pastry dough
1 cup	hazelnuts
1/3 cup	granulated sugar
1 cup	flour, more if needed
1/2 cup	unsalted butter, more for tart pan
1	egg

ORDER OF WORK

1 MAKE THE HAZELNUT PASTRY DOUGH

2 BAKE THE HAZELNUT PASTRY

3 ASSEMBLE THE TART

1 MAKE THE HAZELNUT PASTRY DOUGH

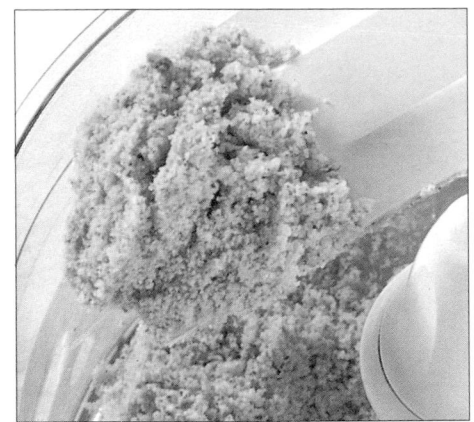

1 Toast and skin the hazelnuts (see box, right). Reserve 8 hazelnuts for garnish. In the food processor, grind the remaining hazelnuts, with the sugar, to a fine powder. Alternatively, grind them with the sugar in 2–3 batches in a blender.

! TAKE CARE !
Do not overwork or the oil from the nuts will create a paste.

HOW TO TOAST AND SKIN NUTS

Toasting nuts intensifies their flavor and adds crunch to their texture. It also loosens the skins from nuts such as hazelnuts for easy removal.

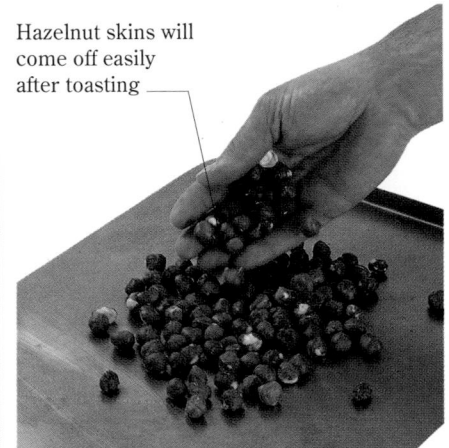

Hazelnut skins will come off easily after toasting

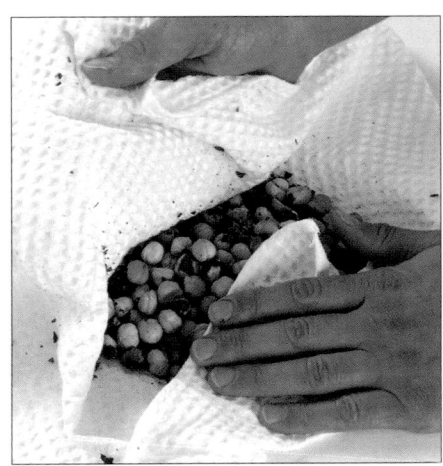

1 Heat the oven to 350°F. Spread the nuts on a baking sheet and toast until lightly browned, stirring occasionally, 12–15 minutes.

2 While the nuts are still hot, rub them in a rough dish towel to remove their skins, then let cool.

2 Sift the flour onto a work surface, add the ground nut mixture, and make a large well in the center.

3 Cut the butter into pieces and add the pieces to the well in the center of the flour.

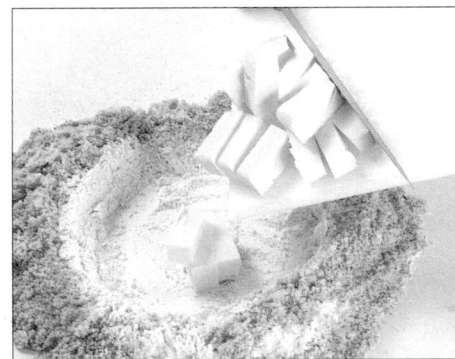

4 Add the egg and, using your fingertips, work the ingredients in the well until soft and thoroughly mixed.

Butter, egg, and sugar are blended with fingertips

5 Draw the hazelnut powder and the flour into the center, using the pastry scraper. Work them into the butter mixture with your fingers to form coarse crumbs.

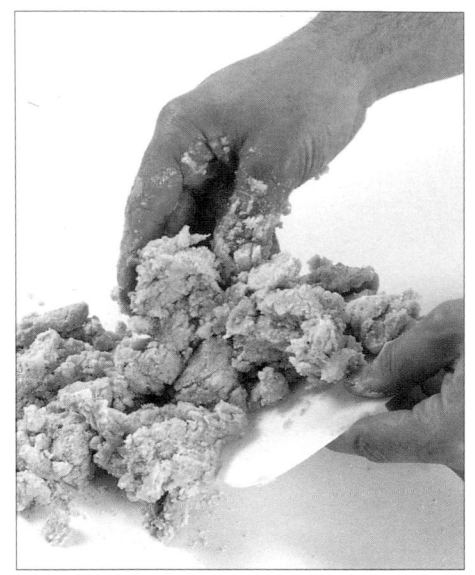

6 Continue working so the crumbs start sticking together. Press the crumbs together with your fingertips to form a ball of dough.

7 Lightly flour the work surface, then blend the dough by pushing it away from you with the heel of your hand. Gather it up and continue to blend until it peels easily from the work surface. Shape into a ball, wrap, and chill until firm, at least 30 minutes.

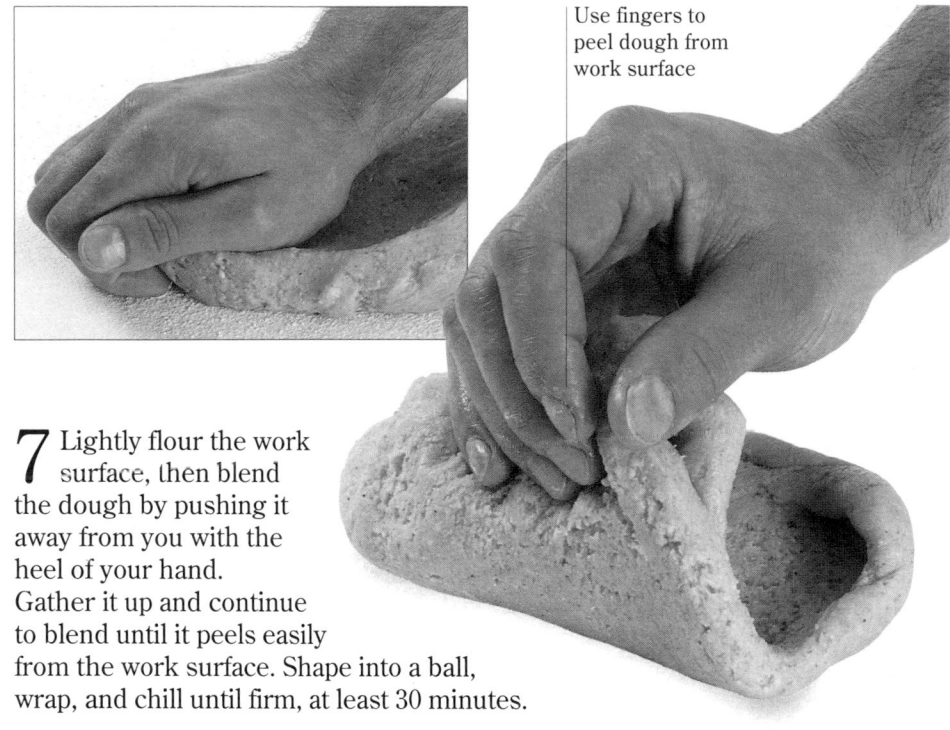

Use fingers to peel dough from work surface

2 BAKE THE HAZELNUT PASTRY

1 Heat the oven to 350°F. Brush the tart pan with melted butter, using the pastry brush.

Brushing pan with butter helps prevent dough sticking

2 With the back of a spoon or the heel of your hand, press the dough into the pan to make an even layer.

3 Chill the dough until firm, at least 15 minutes. Bake in the heated oven until the pastry is golden brown and shrinking slightly from the side of the pan, 30–35 minutes.

ANNE SAYS
"Baking the pastry until golden gives the hazelnuts a full toasted flavor."

4 Set the tart pan on the top of a bowl so the side will loosen. Transfer the pastry round on the base of the pan to a serving plate. Let cool.

3 ASSEMBLE THE TART

1 Make the Marsala whipped cream: using the whisk, whip the heavy cream in a chilled bowl until it forms soft peaks.

Flavorings are added when cream is still soft

2 Add the confectioners' sugar and Marsala. Continue whipping until the cream forms stiff peaks.

Chilled bowl helps give volume to whipped cream

3 Pick over the raspberries. Hull the strawberries, and wash them only if they are dirty.

Moist green hull indicates freshness

Tip of knife scoops hull from strawberry

4 With the small knife, cut the strawberries in half, or into quarters if they are large.

5 Using the metal spatula, spread two-thirds of the Marsala whipped cream evenly over the cooled hazelnut pastry, just to the edge.

! TAKE CARE !
Washing softens strawberries, so only wash them if absolutely necessary.

Pastry bag is twisted over thumb to control flow of Marsala cream

6 Starting at the outer edge and working inward, arrange the strawberries in concentric circles on the Marsala whipped cream. Arrange the raspberries in a pile in the center of the cream, leaving about 1/2-inch space between the strawberries and raspberries for piping rosettes.

7 Put the rest of the Marsala cream into the pastry bag fitted with the star tube. Pipe a ring of cream rosettes between the strawberries and raspberries, and 8 large rosettes around the outside edge, on the strawberries. Place 1 reserved hazelnut in the center of each rosette. Chill until serving.

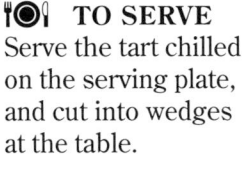 **TO SERVE**
Serve the tart chilled on the serving plate, and cut into wedges at the table.

Toasted hazelnut pastry makes a crunchy base for berry and cream tart

Marsala wine in rosettes of whipped cream gives an Italian touch to fruit tart

Hazelnut garnish indicates flavoring in pastry

VARIATION

STRAWBERRY TART WITH CHOCOLATE CREAM

Here, in Crostata di Fragole al Cioccolato, *a layer of rich chocolate cream is spread on an almond pastry base to make a perfect background for a topping of fresh strawberries. Raspberries can be substituted for the strawberries, if you like.*

Strawberries arranged in concentric circles make attractive topping

1 Make the pastry dough as directed in the main recipe, substituting ³/₄ cup whole blanched almonds for the hazelnuts. Bake as directed.
2 Chop ¹/₄ lb semisweet chocolate into small chunks.

3 Omit the Marsala whipped cream. Put ¹/₂ cup heavy cream and the chopped chocolate in a medium saucepan and heat, stirring occasionally with a wooden spoon, until the chocolate is melted and smooth, 3–5 minutes. Let cool slightly, then refrigerate just until cold, stirring occasionally.

4 While the chocolate cream is chilling, hull 1 quart strawberries, washing them only if dirty, and cut them in half, or in quarters if large. Omit the raspberries.
5 Using an electric beater or a whisk, beat the chilled chocolate cream until fluffy and light in color, 3–5 minutes. Do not overbeat the mixture or it may separate, becoming grainy.
6 With a metal spatula, spread the chocolate cream over the cooled almond pastry to form a smooth, even layer.

7 Arrange the strawberries, cut-side down, in concentric circles, on top of the chocolate cream.
8 Cut the tart into wedges and serve on individual plates.

Crisp almond base contrasts with smooth chocolate

RICOTTA CHEESECAKE

Crostata di Ricotta

🍴 SERVES 8–10 🥄 WORK TIME 35–40 MINUTES* 🍲 BAKING TIME 1–1¼ HOURS

EQUIPMENT

9- to 10-inch springform pan

strainer

chef's knife

pastry brush

bowls

small knife

grater

wooden spoon

rolling pin

parchment paper

pastry scraper

baking sheet

chopping board

ANNE SAYS
"*A springform cake pan is necessary because the cheesecake cannot be inverted for removal from the pan after baking.*"

When I first tasted a classic Italian cheesecake of fresh ricotta flavored with candied orange peel and almonds, baked in a sweet lemon pastry crust, I knew that this was perfection. The fresher the cheese, the better the cake.

GETTING AHEAD

The cheesecake can be made up to 1 day ahead and kept refrigerated. The flavor will mellow, but the texture will not be as light.

*plus 45–60 minutes chilling time

SHOPPING LIST

1	orange
2 tbsp	chopped candied orange peel
2½ lb	ricotta cheese
½ cup	sugar
1 tbsp	flour
	salt
1 tsp	vanilla extract
¼ cup	golden raisins
¼ cup	slivered almonds
4	egg yolks
	For the sweet pastry dough
¾ cup	unsalted butter, more for cake pan
2 cups	flour, more if needed
1	lemon
¼ cup	sugar
4	egg yolks
1	whole egg, for glaze

INGREDIENTS

orange

ricotta cheese

vanilla extract

unsalted butter

lemon

flour

golden raisins

candied orange peel

egg yolks

slivered almonds

whole egg

sugar

ORDER OF WORK

1 MAKE THE SWEET PASTRY DOUGH

2 ROLL OUT DOUGH AND LINE THE PAN

3 MAKE THE FILLING

4 MAKE THE LATTICE AND BAKE THE CHEESECAKE

1 MAKE THE SWEET PASTRY DOUGH

1 Using the rolling pin, pound the butter between 2 sheets of parchment paper to soften it slightly.

ANNE SAYS
"*It is important that the well in the flour is made large enough so that the ingredients can be mixed together easily.*"

Softened butter will blend easily with sugar

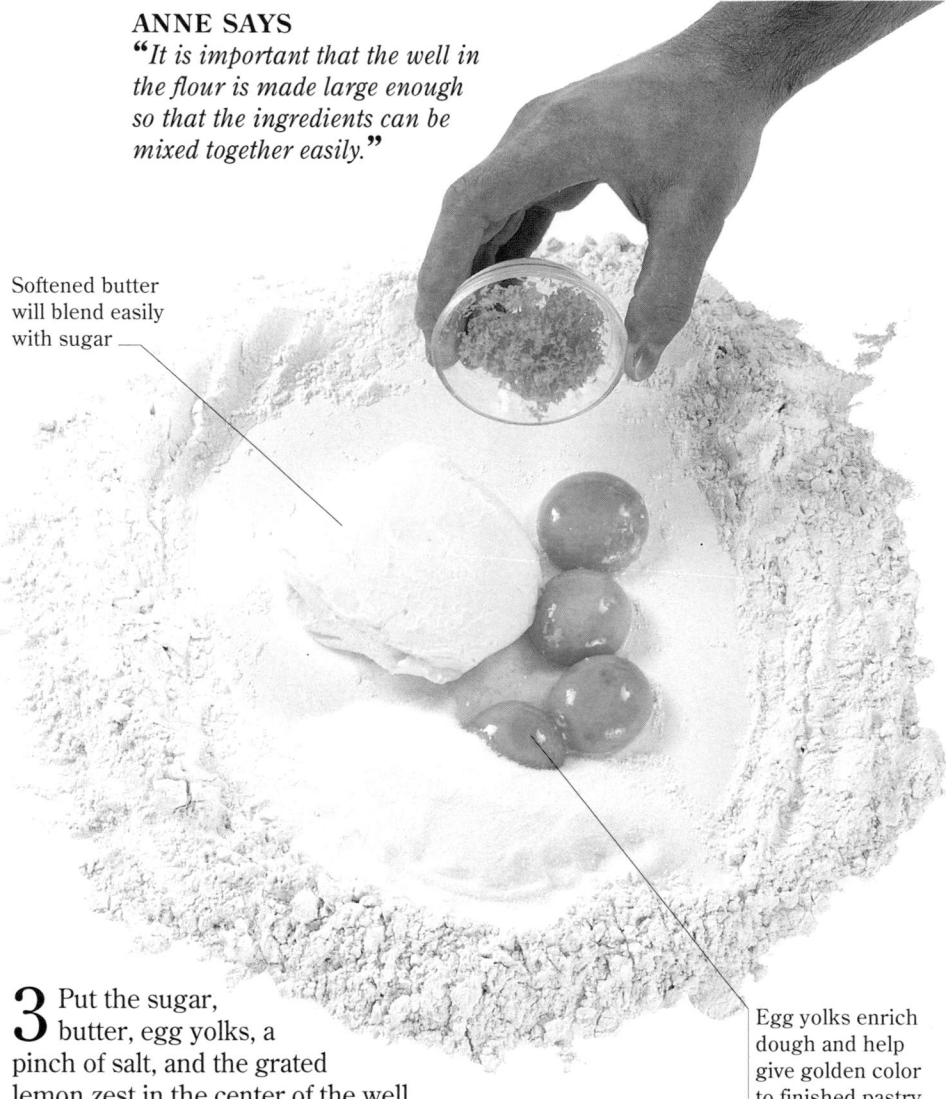

Egg yolks enrich dough and help give golden color to finished pastry

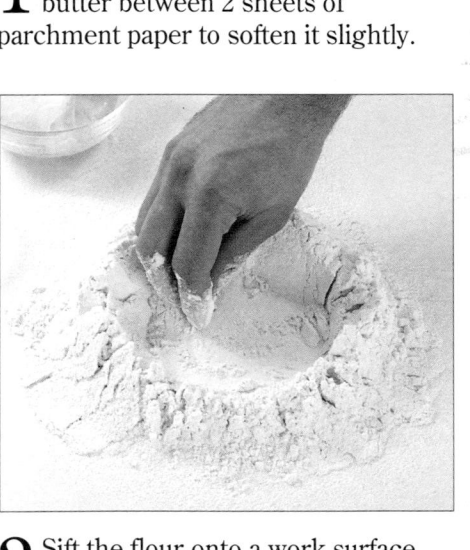

2 Sift the flour onto a work surface and make a large well in the center. Grate the zest from the lemon.

3 Put the sugar, butter, egg yolks, a pinch of salt, and the grated lemon zest in the center of the well.

Work butter with egg yolk and sugar

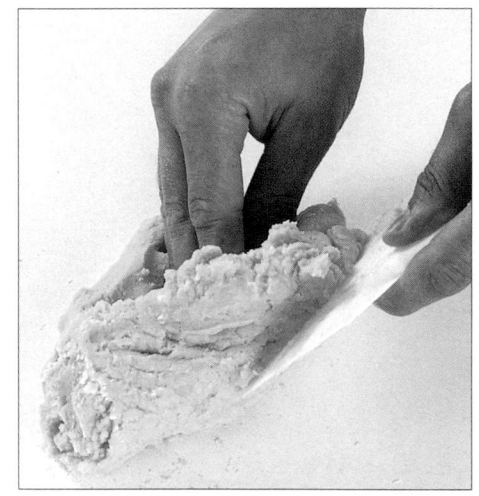

4 Using your fingertips, work together all the ingredients in the well until they are thoroughly mixed.

5 Gradually draw in the flour with the pastry scraper. Work the flour into the other ingredients. Press the dough into a ball.

6 Lightly flour the work surface, then blend the dough by pushing it away from you with the heel of your hand. Gather the dough up with the pastry scraper and continue to blend until the dough is very smooth and peels away from the work surface in one piece, 1–2 minutes.

Kneading distributes fat evenly throughout dough

ANNE SAYS
"After kneading the dough 1–2 minutes it should be as smooth as putty."

7 Shape the dough into a ball, wrap it, and chill it in the refrigerator until firm, about 30 minutes.

2 ROLL OUT DOUGH AND LINE THE PAN

1 Brush the bottom and side of the springform pan with melted butter. Lightly flour the work surface and roll out three-quarters of the dough to make a 14- to 15-inch round.

2 Roll up the dough around the rolling pin, then unroll it loosely so that it drapes over the prepared pan.

3 Lift the edge of the dough with one hand and press it well into the bottom of the pan with the other hand. Press the dough gently up the side of the pan with your fingers.

4 Using a table knife, trim excess dough even with the outer edge of the pan. Chill the shell, together with the remaining dough and trimmings, 15 minutes. Meanwhile, make the filling.

Side of dough shell should be level with pan edge

3 MAKE THE FILLING

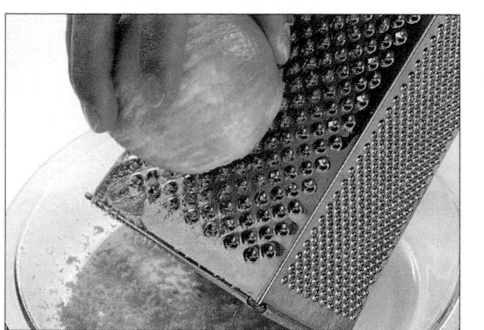

1 Grate the zest from the orange onto a small plate. Finely chop the candied orange peel.

2 Place the ricotta in a large bowl and, beat in the sugar, flour, and 1/2 tsp salt.

3 Add the grated orange zest, chopped candied peel, vanilla extract, golden raisins, slivered almonds, and egg yolks to the ricotta. Beat the mixture together thoroughly to combine.

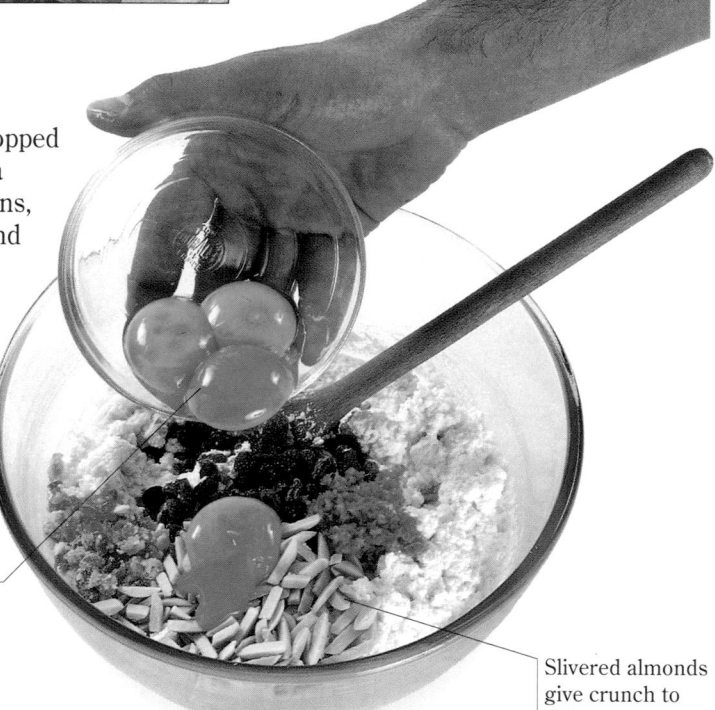

Egg yolks will bind cheese mixture so it sets during baking

Slivered almonds give crunch to filling

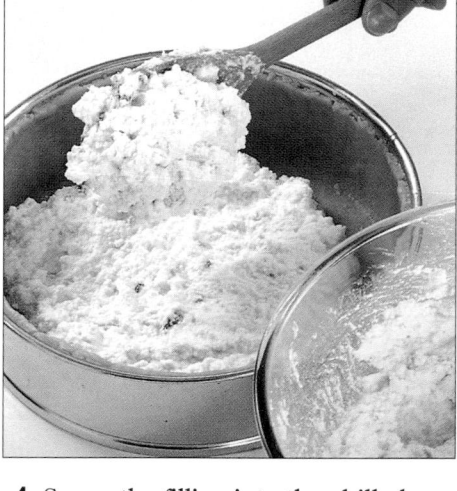

4 Spoon the filling into the chilled pastry shell. Tap the pan on the work surface to eliminate any air pockets. Smooth the top of the filling, using the back of the wooden spoon.

4 MAKE THE LATTICE AND BAKE THE CHEESECAKE

1 Press any dough trimmings into the remaining one-quarter of the dough and roll it into a 10-inch round on a lightly floured surface. Using the chef's knife, cut the dough into strips about 1/2-inch wide.

Alternate strips are folded back

2 Lay half of the strips, left to right, across the filling, about 3/4 inch apart, so any ends hang over the edge of the pan. Fold back alternate strips halfway. Set a new strip across the strips in the center of the filling.

Lay strips loosely over filling so they do not shrink during baking

Ends are left to hang over edge of pan

3 Unfold the folded strips to cover the crosswise strip, again leaving ends to hang over the edge of the pan.

4 Fold back the alternate strips. Place the next crosswise strip about ³/₄ inch from the first.

Weave dough strips in symmetrical pattern

Dough strips should be even

5 Cover the second crosswise strip by unfolding the folded strips across it. Continue to fold back alternate strips as before.

6 Repeat with a third crosswise strip. By this stage, half of the surface should be latticed.

7 Turn the pan 180° and repeat the process on the other half of the cheesecake, in the same way, so the whole cake is latticed.

Interwoven lattice looks appealing on top of cheesecake

8 With the small knife, carefully trim off the overhanging ends of dough, so that the pastry dough strips are even with the edge of the pastry shell.

9 Make an egg glaze: lightly beat the whole egg with $1/2$ tsp salt. Moisten the ends of the strips with the glaze, then seal them to the edge. Brush the lattice with the glaze and chill the cheesecake until firm, 15–30 minutes. Heat the oven to 350°F and put the baking sheet near the bottom of the oven.

Remove side of pan when cake has cooled so that cake becomes firm

10 Bake the cheesecake on the heated baking sheet until the top is firm and golden brown, 1–1$1/4$ hours. Let the cake cool in its pan until just warm, then remove the side of the pan and let the cake cool completely.

TO SERVE
Transfer the cheesecake to a large serving plate. Cut into wedges and serve at room temperature.

Lattice topping is characteristic of Italian *crostate*

Smooth ricotta filling contrasts with crisp lemon pastry

VARIATION
CHOCOLATE RICOTTA PIE
I discovered this delicious Crostata di Ricotta al Cioccolato, *in a pastry shop in Assisi.*

1 Make the sweet pastry dough as directed in the main recipe, with 1$1/2$ cups flour, 3 egg yolks, 3 tbsp sugar, and $1/2$ cup butter; omit the lemon zest.
2 Roll out all the pastry dough to line a 13-x 9-x 2-inch buttered baking dish. The pastry dough crust should be about 1$1/4$ inches high around the sides.
3 Using a chef's knife, finely chop $1/4$ lb semisweet chocolate; alternatively, chop it in a food processor, using the pulse button.
4 Make the filling as directed, adding the chopped chocolate and grated orange zest in place of the candied fruit, golden raisins, and almonds.
5 Fill the prepared pastry dough shell, chill, and bake as directed until set, 35–40 minutes. Let the pie cool completely, in the baking dish.
6 Chop 1 oz more chocolate. Melt it in a bowl set in a saucepan of hot water, stirring until the chocolate is smooth. Stir in $1/2$ tsp vegetable oil.
7 Dip the tines of a fork in the melted chocolate and flick over the top of the pie so that the chocolate makes a freeform lattice.
8 Cut the pie into bars and serve on individual plates.

WALNUT CAKE WITH CARAMEL TOPPING

Torta di Noci

🍽 SERVES 8　🥄 WORK TIME 25–30 MINUTES　🍲 BAKING TIME 1–1¼ HOURS

EQUIPMENT

food processor

bowls

wire rack

medium saucepan

parchment paper

whisk

kitchen scissors

pastry brush

metal spatula

grater

pencil

rubber spatula

metal skewer

wooden spoon

9-inch round cake pan

A crisp layer of caramel tops this rich walnut cake flavored with grappa or rum – fare for a celebration, but surprisingly simple to make.

GETTING AHEAD

The cake can be stored up to 2 days in an airtight container; the flavor will mellow. Add the caramel topping just before serving because it softens on standing.

SHOPPING LIST

1	lemon
2	slices of white bread
1½ cups	walnut halves (6 oz)
4	eggs
½ cup	unsalted butter, more for cake pan
⅔ cup	sugar
2 tbsp	grappa
	For the topping
¼ cup	water
½ cup	sugar

INGREDIENTS

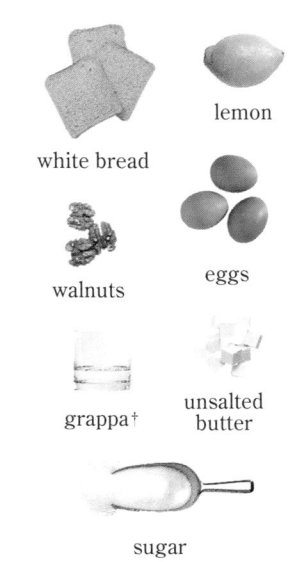

lemon

white bread

walnuts

eggs

grappa†

unsalted butter

sugar

†rum can also be used

ANNE SAYS

"Grappa is the Italian equivalent of marc, a spirit made by distilling the remains of white grapes that have been crushed to make wine. It may be flavored with herbs."

ORDER OF WORK

1 PREPARE AND BAKE THE CAKE

2 MAKE THE TOPPING AND COAT THE CAKE

1 PREPARE AND BAKE THE CAKE

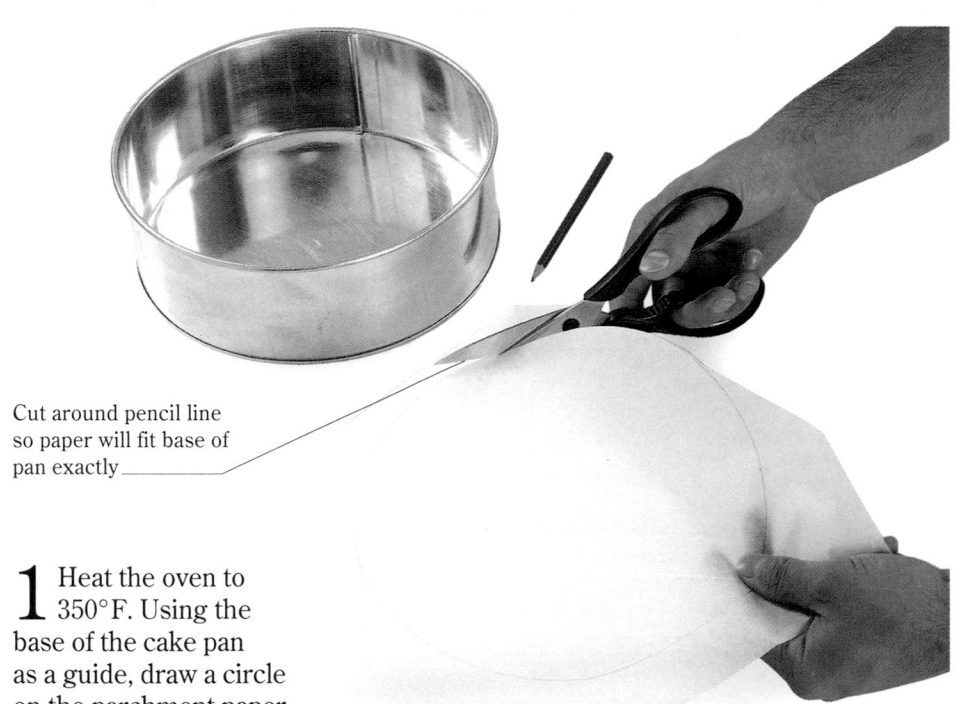

Cut around pencil line so paper will fit base of pan exactly

1 Heat the oven to 350°F. Using the base of the cake pan as a guide, draw a circle on the parchment paper and cut it out.

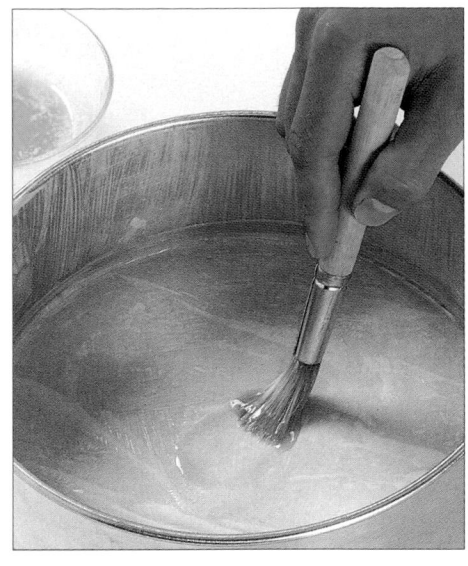

2 Brush the bottom and side of the cake pan with melted butter and line the bottom with the parchment paper round. Brush the paper with more melted butter.

Walnuts and crumbs give cake its characteristic texture

Dryness of bread helps prevent nuts becoming oily when they are ground

3 Grate the zest from the lemon. Toast the bread in the heated oven until very dry, 5–7 minutes; do not let it brown. Break the bread into pieces and put them in the food processor. Work until finely ground, using the pulse button. Alternatively, grind the bread in a rotary cheese grater.

4 Reserve 8 walnut halves for garnish. Add the remaining walnuts to the food processor and grind until quite fine. Alternatively, finely chop the nuts with a chef's knife.

! TAKE CARE !
Do not overwork the nuts in the processor or they will form a paste. You may like to leave a few chunks for texture.

5 Separate the eggs (see page 105). Cream the butter using the wooden spoon or an electric mixer. Add two-thirds of the sugar and beat until light and fluffy, 2–3 minutes.

Wooden spoon or electric mixer can be used for creaming

Butter is creamed before sugar is added so that sugar will be easy to incorporate

6 Add the egg yolks, one at a time, to the creamed butter and sugar, beating well after each addition.

7 Add the grated lemon zest and grappa, and stir into the batter.

ANNE SAYS
"Beat the batter well to develop the flavor in the lemon zest."

8 Add the ground walnuts and breadcrumbs to the batter and stir well to combine.

9 Whisk the egg whites until stiff (see box, page 106). Sprinkle with the remaining sugar and whisk until glossy, about 20 seconds longer. Gently fold one-quarter of the egg whites into the batter.

Cut and fold meringue into batter

Add heavier
mixture to
lighter one
when folding

10 Add the egg white and walnut mixture to the remaining egg whites. Cut down into the center of the bowl, scoop under the contents, and turn them over in a rolling motion. At the same time, turn the bowl counter clockwise.

11 Spoon the batter into the prepared cake pan and smooth the top with the rubber spatula. Bake in the heated oven until the metal skewer inserted in the center of the cake comes out clean, 1–1¼ hours.

Buttered paper
is easy to peel
from cake

12 Let the cake cool slightly, then invert it onto the wire rack. Peel off and discard the paper, and let the cake cool completely.

Wire rack lets
air circulate

HOW TO SEPARATE EGGS

Eggs are easy to separate if you use the shell. However, if an egg shell is contaminated with salmonella, bacteria can cling to the shell and spread. Alternative methods are filtering the white through your fingers or using an egg separator.

1 **To separate an egg with the shell:** crack the egg at its broadest point by tapping it against a bowl. With 2 thumbs, break it open, letting some white slip over the edge of the shell into the bowl.

2 Tip the yolk from one half of the shell to the other, detaching the remaining white from the yolk. If yolk slips into the white, remove it with the shell. To remove white threads, pinch them against the side of the shell with your fingers.

To separate an egg with your fingers: crack the egg into a bowl. Hold your cupped fingers over another bowl and let the white fall through them, leaving the yolk.

HOW TO WHISK EGG WHITES UNTIL STIFF

Egg whites should be whisked until stiff but not dry. In order for them to whisk properly, the bowl and whisk must be completely free from any trace of water, grease, or egg yolk. A copper bowl and a large balloon whisk are the classic French utensils for whisking egg whites. A metal or glass bowl with a balloon whisk or an electric mixer can also be used.

1 Begin whisking whites slowly. When they become foamy and white, increase the whisking speed. If you like, add a small pinch of salt or cream of tartar to help achieve maximum volume.

! TAKE CARE !
Do not slow down the whisking once the whites form soft peaks or they may "turn", becoming grainy.

2 The whites are whisked enough if they form a stiff peak when the whisk is lifted, gathering in the whisk wires and sticking without falling. The whites should be used at once because they quickly separate on standing.

! TAKE CARE !
Do not overbeat the egg whites; if they are overbeaten, the correct texture cannot be reconstituted.

2 MAKE THE TOPPING AND COAT THE CAKE

1 Heat the water and sugar in the saucepan over low heat until the sugar has dissolved. Boil, without stirring, until the syrup starts to turn golden.

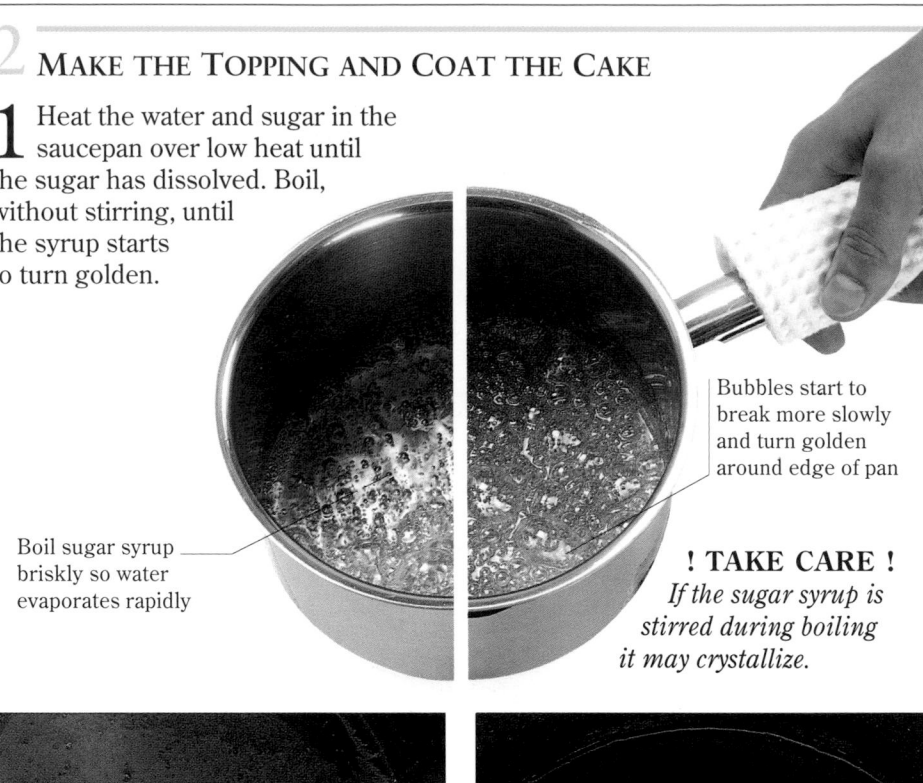

Boil sugar syrup briskly so water evaporates rapidly

Bubbles start to break more slowly and turn golden around edge of pan

! TAKE CARE !
If the sugar syrup is stirred during boiling it may crystallize.

2 Lower the heat and continue cooking, swirling the syrup in the pan once or twice so it colors evenly.

3 Cook until the caramel is deep golden in color for best flavor. Do not overcook or caramel may burn.

Protect hand with dish towel from hot handle and rising steam

Cold water will quickly cool base of pan

4 Quickly, plunge the base of the pan into a bowl of cold water to stop the caramel cooking.

Hold metal spatula at an angle when spreading caramel

Spread caramel quickly because it sets as soon as it is cool

5 As soon as the caramel has stopped bubbling, pour it over the cake. Using the metal spatula, spread the caramel quickly in a thin layer. Immediately arrange the reserved walnut halves on top of the cake.

🍴 TO SERVE

Transfer the cake to a serving plate and cut into 8 even-sized portions with a sharp knife.

Cake is cut into neat serving portions

Walnut halves are set into caramel topping

VARIATION

WALNUT CAKE WITH RAISINS

Torta di Noci e Uve Passe packs an added punch: the raisins are soaked in grappa.

1 Put 1 cup dark raisins in a small, shallow bowl. Add ½ cup grappa and let stand 15 minutes.

2 Drain the raisins and reserve the grappa. Make the cake as directed in the main recipe, using all the walnuts for the batter and adding the raisins with the lemon zest. Bake as directed.

3 While the cake is still warm, spoon on the reserved grappa.

4 Omit the caramel topping. Cut 4 or 5 strips of light cardboard about ³/₄-inch wide and lay them on top of the cake. Sift confectioners' sugar evenly over the cake. Carefully lift off the strips and discard the excess sugar.

5 Lay the strips back on the cake to make a diagonal lattice and cover again with sifted confectioners' sugar; you will need about ½ cup in total. Again, carefully lift off the cardboard strips.

6 Transfer the cake to a serving plate and serve.

GRAPEFRUIT GRANITA

Granita di Pompelmo

🍽 SERVES 4　🥄 WORK TIME 15–20 MINUTES　❄ FREEZING TIME 5–6 HOURS*

EQUIPMENT

chef's knife

whisk

small saucepan

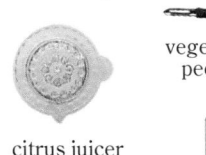

vegetable peeler

citrus juicer

small strainer

non-metallic bowl

parchment paper †

chopping board

† wax paper can also be used

ANNE SAYS
"*In this recipe, a whisk is used to break up the ice, but you can also make granita using a food processor or blender: pour the grapefruit mixture into ice cube trays and freeze until set, 2–3 hours. When frozen, transfer the ice cubes to a food processor or blender and work until slushy.*"

Grapefruit granita, served here with All Souls' Day almond cookies, is a refreshing end to a rich dinner. Sweetened grapefruit and lemon juices are put directly in the freezer and frozen into a granita. Unlike a smooth sorbet, the texture of a granita should resemble coarse snow – instead of using a churn, this effect is achieved by whisking the fruit juice and sugar mixture at hourly intervals, to break up the ice crystals as they form.

GETTING AHEAD

The granita can be made up to 2 days ahead and kept in the freezer. If the ice mixture has solidified, leave it at room temperature until slushy. Whisk it and refreeze 30–60 minutes, or grind it in a food processor just before serving.

* stir mixture about once an hour

SHOPPING LIST

3	medium grapefruit
1/2	lemon
1/4 cup	sugar, more to taste
2 tbsp	water
	All Souls' Day almond cookies (see box, page 110) for serving (optional)

INGREDIENTS

grapefruit

lemon

sugar

almond cookies (optional)

ANNE SAYS
"*Pink grapefruit will give the granita a pretty color, but as these grapefruit are sweeter than white grapefruit, you may need to reduce the sugar slightly.*"

ORDER OF WORK

1 MAKE AND FREEZE THE GRAPEFRUIT GRANITA

2 MAKE THE CANDIED GRAPEFRUIT ZEST AND SERVE THE GRANITA

1 MAKE AND FREEZE THE GRAPEFRUIT GRANITA

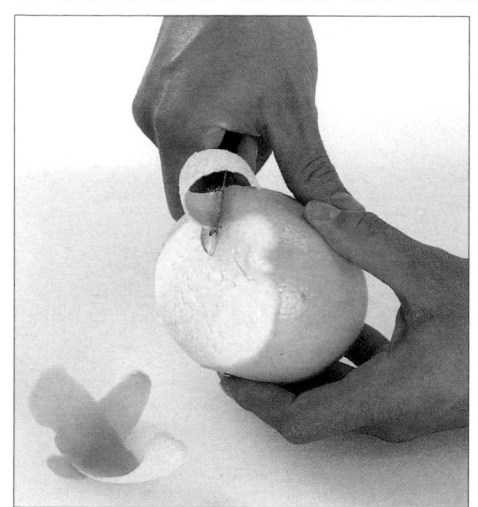

1 Thinly pare the zest from half of 1 grapefruit, leaving behind the white pith. Reserve the pared zest.

Pale yellow grapefruit juice makes delicate-colored granita

2 Squeeze the juice from all of the grapefruit, and pour into a measuring cup; you should have about 2 cups juice.

ANNE SAYS
"*To extract maximum juice, roll the grapefruit firmly on the work surface with the palm of your hand.*"

3 Strain the juice into the non-metallic bowl. Squeeze the juice from the lemon, and strain into the grapefruit juice. Add half of the sugar, and stir until dissolved. Taste, adding more sugar if you like.

Strain grapefruit and lemon juices to remove any seeds and small pieces of pulp

4 Freeze the liquid until ice starts to form on top, 45–60 minutes. Whisk to break the ice.

5 Continue freezing, whisking the mixture to break the ice about once an hour, until the granita is slushy and slightly granular. Allow 4–5 hours.

2 MAKE THE CANDIED GRAPEFRUIT ZEST AND SERVE THE GRANITA

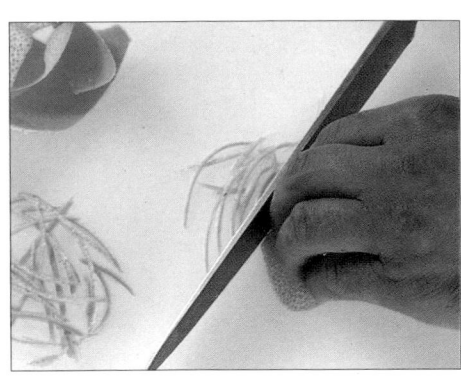

1 With the chef's knife, cut the pared grapefruit zest into very fine julienne strips.

2 In the small saucepan, heat the remaining 2 tbsp sugar with the water until the sugar has dissolved. Add the grapefruit zest.

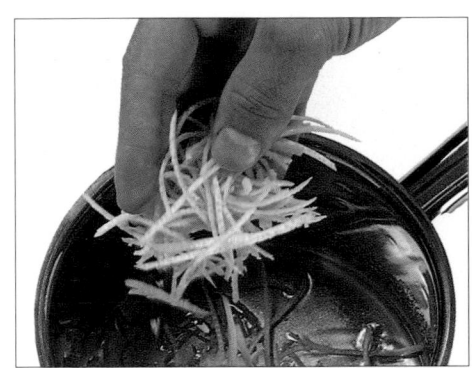

ALL SOULS' DAY ALMOND COOKIES

Chewy and moist, these almond cookies – Fave dei Morti *– are a tradition on All Souls' Day in Italy. They are delicious with granita and other iced desserts, or just as a snack with coffee. The cookies can be stored up to 1 week in an airtight container.*

1 Heat the oven to 350°F. Brush a baking sheet with a little melted butter. Sprinkle with flour and discard the excess. Grate the zest from the lemon. Sift the flour, and whisk the egg.

2 Mix together the ground almonds, sugar, brandy, flour, butter, and lemon zest. Add the egg; stir until the dough holds together and does not stick to the bowl.

3 Wet your hands and roll the dough into 1-inch balls. Place on the prepared baking sheet, leaving 1 inch between the cookies.

🍴 MAKES 24–30

🥣 WORK TIME 15–20 MINUTES

🍲 BAKING TIME 15–20 MINUTES

Gaps are left between cookies to allow for spreading during baking

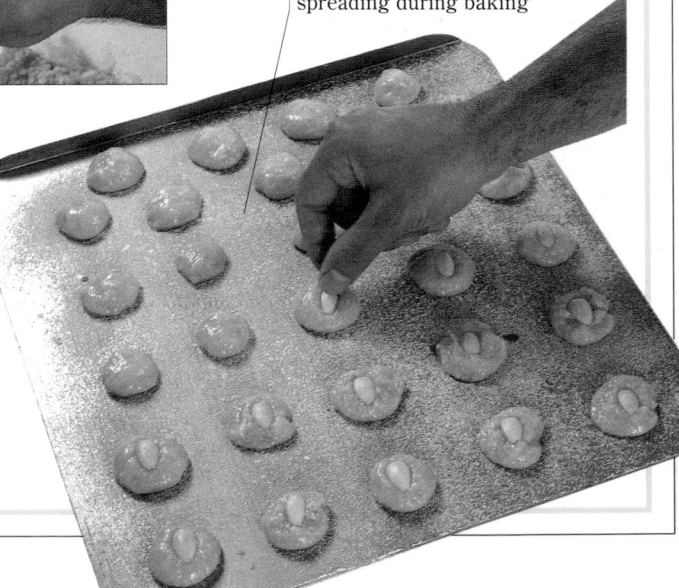

SHOPPING LIST

1	lemon
3/4 cup	flour, more for baking sheet
1	egg
1 cup	ground almonds
2/3 cup	sugar
1 tbsp	brandy
1 tbsp	butter, more for baking sheet
12–15	whole, blanched almonds

4 Split the whole almonds in half, and press a half into the top of each cookie. Bake toward the top of the heated oven until lightly browned, 15–20 minutes. Remove from the oven; let cool 5 minutes before transferring to a wire rack to cool completely.

3 Simmer the zest until all the water has evaporated and the zest is translucent and tender, 12–15 minutes.

4 Spread the grapefruit zest on a sheet of parchment paper with a fork, and let it cool.

5 Spoon the grapefruit granita into 4 chilled coupe glasses. Pile the candied zest on top and serve at once. If you like, All Souls' Day almond cookies can be served on the side.

Use chilled spoon, and work as fast as possible because granita melts quickly

Coupe glasses must be well chilled or granita may melt

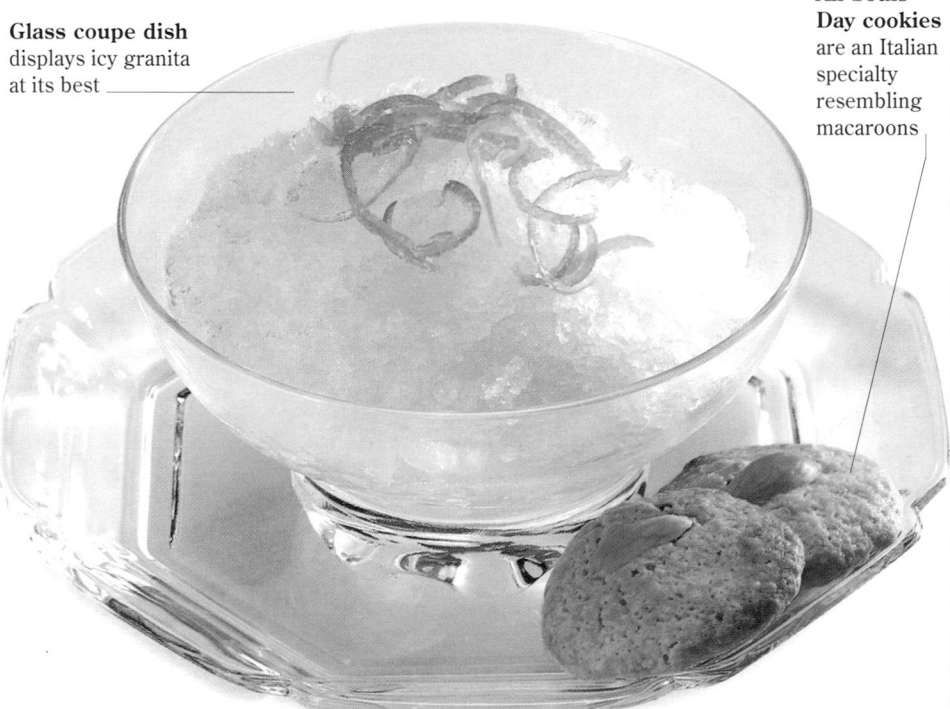

Glass coupe dish displays icy granita at its best

All Souls' Day cookies are an Italian specialty resembling macaroons

VARIATION

COFFEE GRANITA

A favorite in Italian cafés, Granita di Caffè *is made from sweetened espresso, topped here with Amaretto-flavored whipped cream. This recipe serves 6 people.*

1 Bring 1 quart water to a boil. Whisk 1 cup ground espresso or dark-roast coffee into the water, cover, and let stand 10 minutes.
2 Pour the mixture through a strainer, then through a coffee filter, and measure 3 cups liquid.
3 Stir 1/2 cup granulated sugar into the coffee until dissolved. Taste, adding more sugar if you like, and let the mixture cool to room temperature. Freeze as directed in the main recipe.
4 Put 6 stemmed glasses in the refrigerator to chill.
5 Using a whisk or electric mixer, whip 1/2 cup heavy cream in a chilled bowl until it forms soft peaks.
6 Add 1 tbsp confectioners' sugar and 1–2 tbsp Amaretto liqueur, and continue whipping until the cream forms stiff peaks.
7 Fill a pastry bag fitted with a medium star tube with the whipped cream.
8 Spoon the coffee granita into the chilled stemmed glasses. Pipe a large rosette of whipped cream on the top of each. If you like, top each rosette with chocolate-covered espresso beans.

APPLE CAKE

Torta di Mele

🍽 SERVES 8   🥄 WORK TIME 20–25 MINUTES   🍲 BAKING TIME 1¼–1½ HOURS

EQUIPMENT

bowls

9- to 10-inch springform pan

melon baller †

thin-bladed knife

pastry brush

small saucepan

vegetable peeler

electric mixer ‡

small knife

grater

strainer

rubber spatula

metal skewer

chopping board

† teaspoon can also be used
‡ wooden spoon can also be used

A firm dessert apple is best for this moist and dense cake, which is perfect for picnics. Any flavorful apple that holds its shape during cooking, such as a Granny Smith, is appropriate. Italian cooks often use Golden Delicious apples, now grown worldwide.

GETTING AHEAD

The cake is best eaten warm from the oven, but it can be stored up to 2 days in an airtight container.

SHOPPING LIST

1½ cups	flour, more for cake pan
½ tsp	salt
1 tsp	baking powder
1	lemon
1¼ lb	apples
¼ cup	unsalted butter, more for cake pan
1 cup	sugar
2	eggs
¼ cup	milk
	For the glaze
¼ cup	water
⅓ cup	sugar

INGREDIENTS

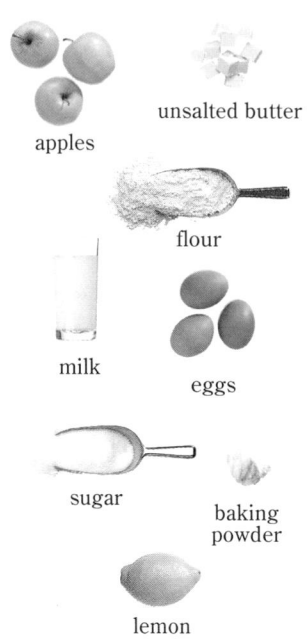

apples

unsalted butter

flour

milk

eggs

sugar

baking powder

lemon

ANNE SAYS
"*Most lemons we buy are coated with wax to prevent loss of moisture, so wash them before grating.*"

ORDER OF WORK

1 MAKE THE CAKE BATTER

2 BAKE THE CAKE AND MAKE THE GLAZE

1 MAKE THE CAKE BATTER

Vegetable peeler removes apple peel easily

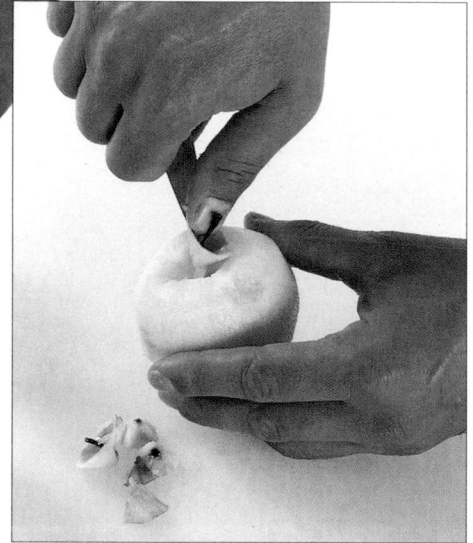

1 Heat the oven to 350°F. Brush the springform pan with melted butter and sprinkle with a little flour, discarding the excess. Sift the measured flour with the salt and baking powder. Grate the zest from the lemon.

2 Peel the apples with the vegetable peeler. Cut the lemon in half and rub the cut surface of the lemon over the apples so that they do not discolor.

3 With the point of the small knife, cut around the stem end of each apple, and remove the stem. Repeat with the flower end.

Slice apples very thinly so they cook quickly

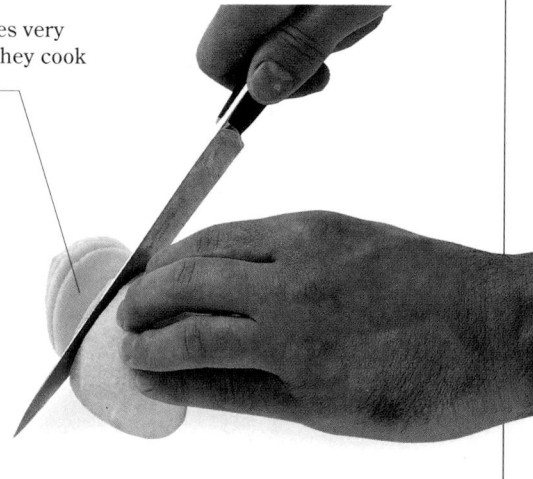

4 Cut the apples lengthwise in half. With the melon baller, carefully scoop out the core and seeds from the center of each apple half, leaving as neat a shape as possible.

5 Set one apple half cut-side down. Cut the apple across into thin slices. Repeat for the other apple halves. Squeeze the remaining juice from the lemon halves over the apple slices.

6 Using the electric mixer, beat the butter in a large bowl until soft and creamy. Add the sugar and grated lemon zest and continue beating until light and crumbly, 2–3 minutes.

7 Add the eggs one by one to the creamed butter and sugar mixture, beating well after each addition.

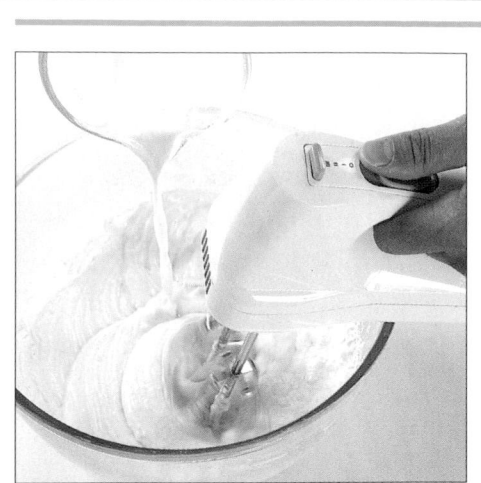

9 Sift in the flour mixture and stir gently with the rubber spatula until evenly mixed. Stir in half of the apple slices.

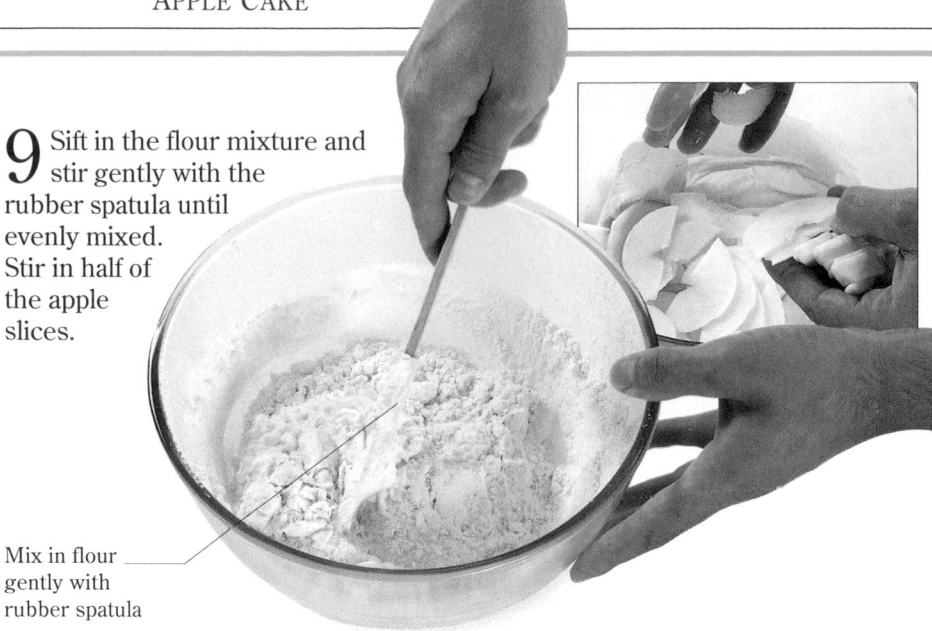

Mix in flour gently with rubber spatula

8 Gradually beat in the milk, and continue beating until the batter is very smooth.

2 BAKE THE CAKE AND MAKE THE GLAZE

1 Spoon the batter into the prepared pan and smooth the top with the rubber spatula.

2 Arrange the remaining apple slices in concentric circles on top of the batter. Bake the cake in the heated oven, 1¼–1½ hours.

Separate apple slices with your fingers when placing them on batter

3 Meanwhile, make the glaze: heat the water and sugar in the small saucepan over low heat until the sugar has dissolved. Bring to a boil and simmer 2 minutes, without stirring, then let cool.

Arrange apple slices neatly for attractive finish

ANNE SAYS
"Be sure to cover the cake completely with the apple slices."

4 The cake is done when it shrinks slightly from the side of the pan and the skewer inserted in the center comes out clean.

Brush glaze over apples while they are hot

5 Brush the sugar syrup glaze on top of the cake as soon as it comes out of the oven. Let the cake cool in the pan.

ANNE SAYS
"The cake will still be moist after it has been baked."

⏵⏺⏴ TO SERVE
Remove the side of the pan, then transfer the cake to a serving plate.

Apple edges are tinged golden

Apple slices in concentric circles glisten with sugar glaze

V A R I A T I O N

PEAR CAKE

Sautéed pears take the place of apples to make this Torta di Pere. *Use firm pears such as Bosc or Anjou.*

1 Butter and flour a 9-inch square cake pan, as directed for Apple Cake.
2 Omit the apples and grated lemon zest. Peel and core 2 lb pears. Cut each pear half into 4 wedges and sprinkle with lemon juice.
3 Heat 2 tbsp butter in a large frying pan or sauté pan, add the pears and sprinkle with 3–4 tbsp sugar. Sauté the pears, turning them once or twice, until golden, 7–10 minutes.
4 Remove the pears with a slotted spoon. Reserve 3–4 wedges. Cut the remaining wedges in 2–3 pieces and let them cool slightly.
5 Prepare the batter as directed, adding 1 tsp vanilla extract to the butter and sugar. Add the pear pieces to the batter and spoon it into the cake pan.
6 Arrange the remaining pear wedges on the surface of the batter in a decorative pattern (they will sink into batter during baking).
7 Bake the cake as directed, 45 minutes only. Omit the sugar syrup glaze.
8 Let the cake cool in the pan, then turn it out onto a piece of aluminum foil and immediately flip the cake onto a serving board.
9 Cut into triangular wedges to serve.

ANNE SAYS
"If you have some syrup left when you have drained the pears it will make a delicious glaze for the baked cake."

WHIPPED CREAM CAKE WITH CHOCOLATE AND NUTS

Zuccotto Toscano

🍽 SERVES 8　　⏱ WORK TIME 45–50 MINUTES*　　♨ BAKING TIME 25–30 MINUTES

EQUIPMENT

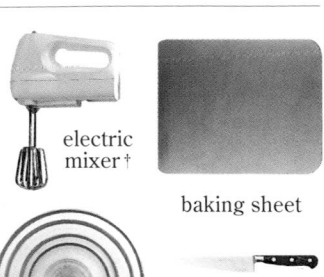

electric mixer †

baking sheet

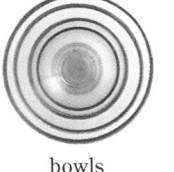

chef's knife

pastry brush

bowls

kitchen scissors

vegetable peeler

thick cardboard

metal spatula

wide spatulas

wire rack

parchment paper ‡

rubber spatula

serrated knife

saucepans

plastic wrap

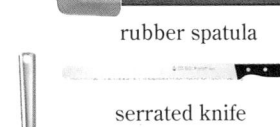

8-inch square cake pan　　strainers

† whisk can also be used
‡ wax paper can also be used

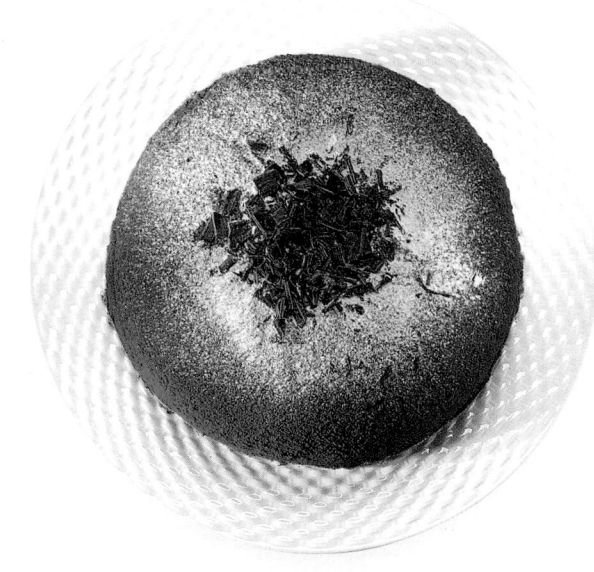

The name zuccotto *derives from* zucca, *meaning pumpkin, a reference to the hemispherical shape of this Florentine specialty, made of sponge cake, cream, and chocolate. You can save time by using 1 lb of store-bought cake.*

plus at least 6 hours chilling time

INGREDIENTS

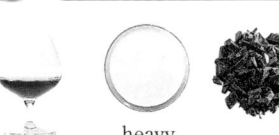

Grand Marnier †

heavy cream

semisweet chocolate

chocolate square

confectioners' sugar

unsalted butter

granulated sugar

flour

eggs

slivered almonds　　cocoa powder

† any other orange-flavored liqueur can also be used

ORDER OF WORK

1 **MAKE THE SPONGE CAKE**

2 **PREPARE THE CHOCOLATE AND NUT FILLING**

3 **ASSEMBLE THE CAKE**

4 **UNMOLD AND DECORATE THE CAKE**

SHOPPING LIST

	For the sponge cake
1/4 cup	unsalted butter, more for cake pan
1 cup	flour, more for cake pan
	salt
4	eggs
2/3 cup	granulated sugar
	oil for bowl
1/3 cup	Grand Marnier
	For the chocolate and nut filling
3/4 cup	slivered almonds
6 oz	semisweet chocolate
2 cups	heavy cream
1/2 cup	confectioners' sugar
	For the decoration
2 tbsp	cocoa powder
2 tsp	confectioners' sugar
1	square of semisweet chocolate

1 MAKE THE SPONGE CAKE

1 Heat the oven to 350°F. Brush the cake pan with melted butter. Line the bottom with a square of parchment paper. Brush the paper with butter, sprinkle the pan with flour, and discard the excess flour.

2 Melt the butter in a small saucepan, and let cool. Meanwhile, sift the flour and a pinch of salt into a bowl.

3 Put the eggs in a large bowl and beat a few seconds just to mix. Beat in the granulated sugar, using the electric mixer.

4 Beat at high speed until the mixture leaves a ribbon trail when the beaters are lifted, 3–5 minutes.

ANNE SAYS
"If using a hand whisk, set the bowl over a saucepan of hot, but not boiling, water and whisk vigorously, about 10 minutes."

5 Sift about one-third of the flour mixture over the egg mixture and fold them together as lightly as possible. Add the remaining flour in the same way in 2 batches.

Transfer cake to rack so steam can escape

6 Just after folding in the last batch of flour, add the cooled, melted butter and fold it in gently but quickly with the rubber spatula.

7 Pour the batter into the prepared cake pan and gently tap the pan on the work surface to level the batter and knock out any air bubbles. Bake at once, near the bottom of the heated oven, until the cake has risen and is firm to the touch when lightly pressed with a fingertip, 25–30 minutes. Remove the cake pan from the oven and leave the oven on.

8 Turn the cake onto the wire rack and peel off the paper. Let the cake cool. Meanwhile, prepare the chocolate and nut filling (see page 118).

2 PREPARE THE CHOCOLATE AND NUT FILLING

1 Spread the almonds on the baking sheet and bake in the heated oven until lightly browned, stirring often so that they color evenly, 8–10 minutes. Do not let them burn or they will be bitter. Let cool completely.

2 With the chef's knife, finely chop the chocolate. Alternatively, chop the chocolate in a food processor, using the pulse button.

ANNE SAYS
"On a warm day, chill the chocolate before you chop it."

Use broad end of knife to chop chocolate, holding tip with other hand

HOW TO WHIP AND SWEETEN CREAM

Heavy cream, with a minimum of 36% butterfat content, is best for whipping, and it should be thoroughly chilled in the refrigerator beforehand. Whipped cream can be covered and refrigerated up to 4 hours. It may separate slightly but will thicken again if whipped briefly.

1 Pour the heavy cream into a chilled medium-sized bowl placed in a larger bowl of ice water.

2 With an electric mixer or whisk, whip until the cream forms soft peaks.

3 Add the sugar and whip until the cream forms soft peaks again and just holds its shape.

4 For stiff peaks, continue whipping until the blades of the mixer or whisk leave clear marks in the cream.

! TAKE CARE !
If overwhipped, the cream will separate and turn to butter. When this is about to happen, it looks granular.

3 Whip the cream with the confectioners' sugar until stiff peaks form (see box, page 118). Fold the toasted almonds with half of the chocolate into the whipped cream. Cover the mixture and chill.

4 Heat the remaining chocolate in a bowl set in a saucepan of hot water, stirring occasionally, just until melted. Leave until cool, but do not let it harden.

3 ASSEMBLE THE CAKE

1 Using the serrated knife, cut the cake into 3 equal triangles. Reserve the 2 small triangles from the sides. Cut each of the large triangles horizontally into 3 layers, to give 9 layers in all.

Slice large triangles of cake to make 9 equal pieces

2 Oil a deep 2-quart non-metallic bowl, and line with 8 triangles of cake, packing them as evenly as possible. Press the triangles deeper into the bowl to close any gaps and make the cake level with the rim. Fill any remaining gaps with trimmings cut to fit. Reserve the remaining triangle shape and trimmings.

Serrated knife is best for slicing cake into layers

Small triangles at sides of square are reserved to fill in gaps and top of cake when molding

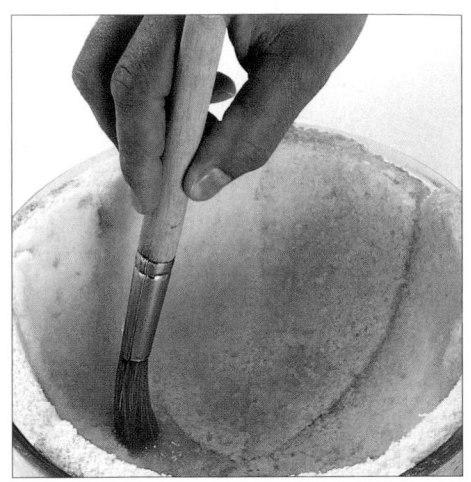

3 If necessary, trim the top edge of the cake even with the rim of the bowl. Brush the cake lining with the Grand Marnier.

4 Spoon half of the whipped cream filling into the cake-lined bowl. With the spoon, spread the filling evenly up the side of the cake lining, leaving a hollow in the middle. Chill in the refrigerator while you prepare the remaining filling.

Use rubber spatula to scrape every last bit of mixture from bowl

5 Add the cooled melted chocolate to the remaining whipped cream and fold until combined.

! TAKE CARE !
If the chocolate is still warm it will melt the cream.

6 Fill the hollow in the middle of the cake with the chocolate cream, smoothing the top with the rubber spatula.

7 Arrange the reserved large triangle over the filling. Cut the reserved small triangles horizontally in half and use to cover the filling completely, together with the reserved trimmings.

8 Cut a round of cardboard slightly smaller than the diameter of the bowl. Set on top of the cake, cover with plastic wrap, and set a 1 lb weight on top. Refrigerate until set, at least 6 hours.

4 UNMOLD AND DECORATE THE CAKE

1 Remove the weight and plastic wrap. Run the metal spatula around the edge of the zuccotto, easing it away from the bowl. Set a board on top of the bowl and invert them. Lift off the bowl.

2 Put the cocoa powder in a small strainer and sprinkle it generously over the zuccotto to cover the cake.

3 Put the confectioners' sugar in the strainer and sprinkle it lightly over the top of the zuccotto. Using the vegetable peeler, shave curls from the square of chocolate. Spoon the curls onto the center of the zuccotto. Using 2 wide spatulas, transfer the cake, with the cardboard round, to a serving plate.

Dusting of cocoa powder gives cake a neat finish

Chocolate curls are a simple but effective garnish

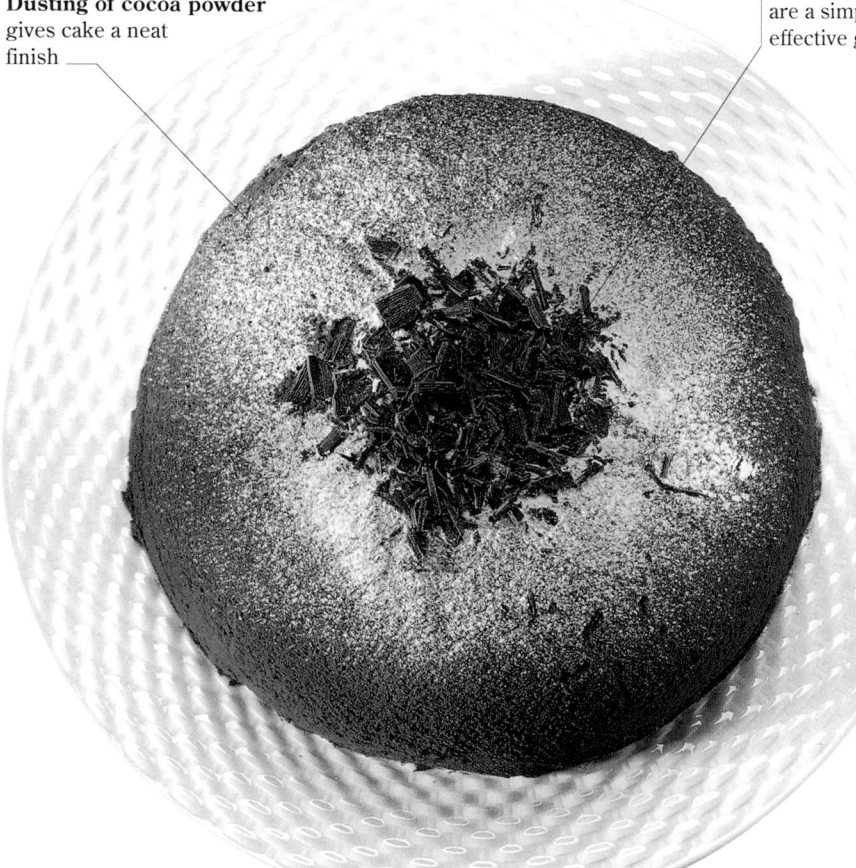

MOCHA WHIPPED CREAM CAKE

Mocha-flavored whipped cream and Amaretti cookies fill this Torta Moka.

1 Make the sponge cake as directed in the main recipe. If necessary, trim any crusty edges from the cake.
2 Using a long serrated knife, cut the cake horizontally into 3 even layers.
3 Brush the cake with Amaretto liqueur instead of Grand Marnier.
4 Omit the almonds and semisweet chocolate. Roughly chop 30 (about 5 oz) Amaretti cookies.
5 Whip the cream as directed, adding 3 tbsp cocoa powder and 1 tbsp instant coffee powder with the confectioners' sugar. Fold in one-third of the chopped Amaretti cookies.
6 Spread a little of the mocha whipped cream mixture on the bottom layer of the cake, top with the middle cake layer, and spread with a little more whipped cream mixture.
7 Cover with the top cake layer and spread the remaining mocha mixture over the top and sides so they are covered. Press the remaining chopped cookies onto the sides. Cut into 8 slices to serve.

GETTING AHEAD

The cake can be made up to 1 day ahead and kept in its covered bowl in the refrigerator. Unmold and decorate no more than 2 hours before serving; keep in a cool place.

ITALIAN KNOW-HOW

EQUIPMENT

A minimum of equipment is required for preparing an Italian meal. First priority is a good set of sharp knives. You won't find a food processor in a traditional Italian kitchen, but in some of the recipes in this book it will save you time chopping and puréeing. A blender can usually be used instead of a food processor, but the ingredients may need to be worked in batches. For cooking pasta, a pot large enough to hold at least 4 quarts of water is essential. Heavy casseroles with lids are indispensable when braising meats such as pork, lamb, and beef on top of the stove or in the oven – use a pan with a thick base to prevent scorching during long, slow cooking.

If you have a pasta machine, now is the time to use it, although with patience you can roll your own pasta by hand. Baking dishes of various shapes and sizes come in handy when preparing many of these recipes. I like to use an attractive baking dish that can be transferred from oven to table, so the food can be served piping hot directly from the dish. Other standard kitchen equipment includes a vegetable peeler, grater, and juicer, as well as wooden spoons, and slotted spoons for lifting foods out of liquid or fat. You will also need a frying pan and a colander or large strainer. A baking sheet is necessary for toasting nuts, and for baking cookies. Some desserts call for a springform pan with a removable side – an easy way to unmold delicate cakes.

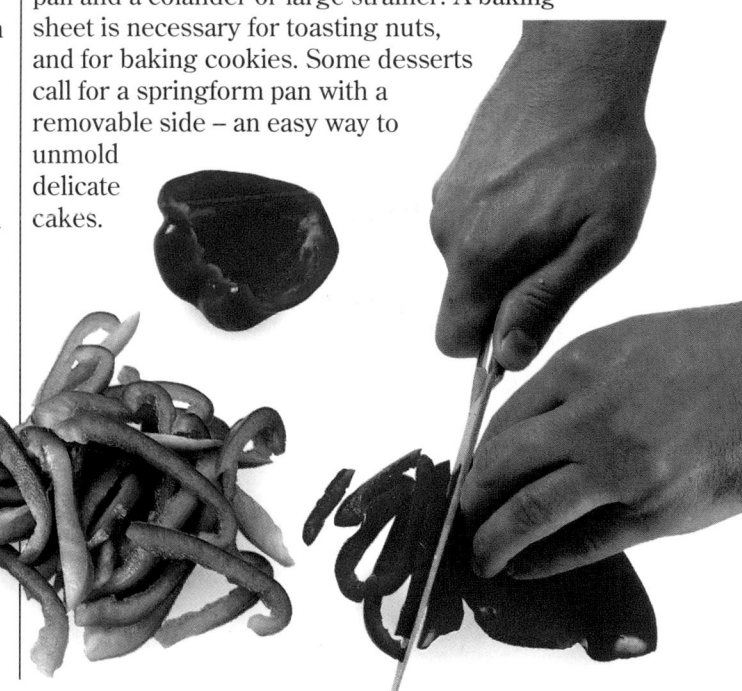

BEEF OR VEAL STOCK

Beef or veal stock is based on raw meat bones that are gently simmered with aromatic vegetables in water. Ask your butcher to cut the bones into pieces. Boiling should be avoided because it makes the stock cloudy.

🍽️ MAKES 2–3 QUARTS

🥣 WORK TIME 20–30 MINUTES

🍲 COOKING TIME 4–5 HOURS

SHOPPING LIST

4–5 lb	beef or veal bones, cut in pieces
2	onions
2	carrots
2	celery stalks
4 quarts	water, more if needed
1	large bouquet garni
10	black peppercorns
1	garlic clove
1 tbsp	tomato paste

1 Heat the oven to 450°F. Put the bones in a large roasting pan and roast until they are well browned, 30–40 minutes, stirring occasionally. Peel and quarter the onions and carrots. Quarter the celery. Add the vegetables to the pan and roast until brown, 15–20 minutes.

2 With a slotted spoon, transfer the bones and vegetables to a stockpot. Discard the fat from the roasting pan and add 2 cups of the water. Bring to a boil, stirring to dissolve the pan juices.

3 Add the liquid to the stockpot with all the remaining ingredients, then add enough water just to cover the bones. Bring slowly to a boil, skimming often with a large metal spoon. As soon as the liquid comes to a boil, lower the heat, and simmer very gently, uncovered, 4–5 hours, skimming occasionally. Add more water, if needed, to keep the bones covered.

4 Strain the stock, then taste it. If the flavor is not strong enough, boil the stock to reduce until concentrated. Remove from the heat, let the stock cool, then chill in the refrigerator. When cold, the fat on the surface will be solid and easy to discard.

Chicken Stock

Chicken stock is an indispensable ingredient in many recipes. Salt and pepper are not added to stock, because it is often reduced in individual recipes to concentrate the flavor. It keeps well up to 3 days, covered, in the refrigerator, or it can be frozen.

🍽 Makes about 2 quarts

🥣 Work Time 15 minutes

🍲 Cooking Time up to 3 hours

Shopping List

2– 2¹/₂ lb	raw chicken backs and necks
1	onion
1	carrot
1	celery stalk
1	bouquet garni
5	peppercorns
2 quarts	water, more if needed

1 Put the chicken in a large saucepan. Quarter the onion, carrot, and celery stalk and add to the pan with the bouquet garni and peppercorns.

2 Add water just to cover the ingredients. Bring to a boil and simmer up to 3 hours, skimming occasionally with a large metal spoon. Add more water if necessary to keep the ingredients covered.

ANNE SAYS
"The longer the chicken stock is simmered, the more flavor it will have."

3 Strain the stock into a large bowl. Cool, then cover, and keep in the refrigerator.

ANNE SAYS
"If you do not make stock at home, buy a good consommé or use bouillon cubes."

Fish Stock

Bones, including the heads and tails, of lean white fish, especially flatfish such as sole, are recommended for fish stock. Avoid oily fish such as mackerel. Fish stock keeps up to 2 days, covered, in the refrigerator, or it can be frozen.

🍽 Makes about 1 quart

🥣 Work Time 10–15 minutes

🍲 Cooking Time 20 minutes

Shopping List

1 lb	fish bones
1	onion
1 cup	dry white wine or juice of ¹/₂ lemon
1 quart	water
3–5	sprigs of parsley
1 tsp	peppercorns

1 Thoroughly wash the fish bones. Cut the bones into 4–5 pieces with a chef's knife. Peel the onion, leaving a little of the root attached, then cut it lengthwise in half. Lay each onion half flat on a chopping board and cut across into thin slices.

2 Put the fish bones in a medium saucepan with the onion slices, dry white wine or lemon juice, water, parsley sprigs, and peppercorns. Bring to a boil and simmer 20 minutes. Skim the stock occasionally with a large metal spoon.

! TAKE CARE !
Do not simmer the fish stock too long or it will have a bitter taste.

3 Strain the stock into a bowl. Let cool, then cover, and keep in the refrigerator.

ANNE SAYS
"I never season stock with salt and ground pepper at the time of making, because it might need to be reduced later in individual recipes, and the flavors will intensify."

INGREDIENTS

Fresh ingredients, particularly vegetables, are the backbone of meals in the Italian countryside. Eggplant, bell peppers, zucchini, artichokes, escarole, and, of course, tomatoes spring at once to mind as typically Italian, but don't forget spinach, carrots, peas, celery, and potatoes as well. They all appear mixed with pasta, braised with meats, as main courses, and as side dishes. Always choose the freshest vegetables available, and buy only those you need so they do not spoil in your refrigerator.

Olive oil is a mainstay – the highest quality unrefined and cold-pressed is at its best added uncooked to dishes such as salads or pasta just before serving. Indeed, on many family tables, a bottle of hearty, cold-pressed olive oil appears as a condiment, much as other countries use salt and pepper. Refined olive oils are less fruity and are lighter in both color and flavor. They are best for sautéing and frying, or in recipes where the olive flavor is not important. Not surprisingly, in light of the climate, a wide array of aromatic herbs such as basil, oregano, flat-leaf parsley, mint, thyme, rosemary, and sage frequently find their way into Italian dishes. Whether they are stirred in at the last minute to donate fresh flavor and color, or added at the beginning of cooking so they blend with other ingredients, herbs are an integral part of Italian cuisine. Equally important is the allium family – onion, garlic, leek, and shallot – while piquant flavorings such as dried red chili pepper, olives, capers, anchovies, vinegar, and lemon juice add a further dimension.

Many Italian recipes are based on cereals and grains. Arborio rice, thicker and shorter than the more familiar long-grain, is best for risotto. Cornmeal (for polenta) and wheat flour are mandatory in any Italian kitchen. Fish, poultry, or meat is usually served as the *secondo piatto*. Flavors are often intensified by the addition of stock or wine. Chicken, beef, and fish stocks add background flavor to dishes, but if the recipe requires slow cooking and strong-flavored ingredients, water can usually be substituted. Marsala, Amaretto, and grappa are also called for in this book.

Cheeses play a significant role in Italian cooking, acting as a main ingredient in cakes, a binder for stuffings, toppings for browning, or simply adding flavor to a dish. Freshly grated Parmesan, semi-soft fontina, blue-veined Gorgonzola, fresh ricotta, and mozzarella are frequently used in the recipes that I have chosen.

When it comes to Italian country desserts, fruits such as apples, pears, strawberries, and raspberries provide natural sweetness, while chocolate, coffee, caramel, and nuts lend their characteristic tastes to cakes and cookies.

ITALIAN COUNTRY COOKING AND YOUR HEALTH

If you are especially concerned about fat content and calories, here are some points to consider when preparing Italian food. Olive oil, a fundamental ingredient in Italian cooking, is high in mono-unsaturated fat and has no cholesterol at all. You are already taking a step in the right direction toward a healthier diet by choosing **Italian Country Cooking**. In addition, grains and vegetables are always present. Whether they are in a simple green salad and a piece of crusty bread or combined, as in Fresh Polenta with Vegetable Stew, they serve to balance the Italian menu. To lower your overall fat intake, look first of all for recipes that rely on ingredients that are naturally low in fat, such as Broiled Mussels with Bell Pepper Topping, and Deviled Chicken. If your concern is cholesterol, turn to dishes in which saturated fat can easily be eliminated or replaced. For instance, use olive oil instead of butter when making Asparagus Risotto and when tossing pasta.

The richness of other recipes can be reduced by leaving out certain ingredients. Omit the meatballs in Baked Rigatoni and the bacon in Quills with Spicy Tomato and Bacon Sauce. Spinach and Potato Gnocchi lend themselves to any sauce, so substitute your favorite vegetable topping for the Tomato-Cream Sauce.

Though rich desserts are hard to resist, large quantities of cream and butter add up to high calories. Choose Grapefruit or Coffee Granita and reduce the sugar, or omit it completely. Use low-fat ricotta cheese. Omit the almonds in the Ricotta Cheesecake and serve thinner slices to satisfy any sweet tooth.

MICROWAVE

Many of these Italian recipes can be adapted for microwave cooking, to speed preparation. Roman-Style Artichokes, for instance, can be cooked in the microwave. Cooking time for Braised Pork with Madeira Sauce can be cut significantly by roasting the meat, tightly covered, in the microwave, then finishing it in a hot oven for a crispy exterior. The lengthy cooking for Beef Braised in Red Wine can also be reduced: brown the beef on top of the stove, then simmer it in the microwave. However, be careful not to add too much liquid and not to cook the beef too long or it will be stringy. You can also save time in other recipes by using the microwave for steaming clams in Broiled Clams, and blanching spinach for Spinach and Potato Gnocchi in Tomato-Cream Sauce and Spinach-Stuffed Veal Rolls (spinach retains its bright green color when cooked in the microwave).

Don't forget that some basic preparations are easy to do in the microwave. For example, you can peel the skin from onions, garlic, and tomatoes: heat onions and garlic cloves at High (100 % power), 45–50 seconds for onions, 15–30 seconds for garlic; put tomatoes in boiling water in a microwave-safe bowl and cook until the skins split, 10–15 seconds. You can also cook bacon, melt chocolate, and even cook caramel in the microwave.

TECHNIQUES

A wide range of basic techniques is illustrated in these recipes, some specifically Italian but others of more general application. You can see how to make fresh pasta and potato gnocchi, and how to cook polenta. There are instructions on how to make a simple tomato sauce, as well as richer cream sauces, and how to clean and cook mussels and clams. To give extra flavor, olive oil, lemon juice, vinegar, and a variety

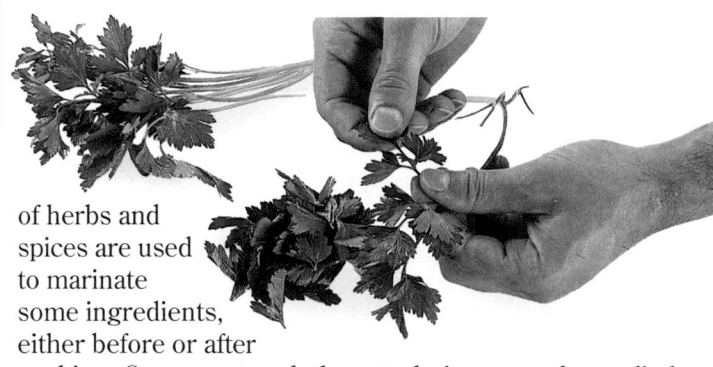

of herbs and spices are used to marinate some ingredients, either before or after cooking. Once mastered, these techniques can be applied to a number of different recipes in this book.

Cooking methods in this book are equally varied, ranging from sautéing chicken in the recipe for Hunter's Chicken to pan-frying fish in Sole Fillets Marinated in Vinegar. Broiling, braising, roasting, and simmering are other important techniques that are covered.

As with other volumes in the *Look & Cook* series, basic techniques are described in detail: how to chop herbs; how to peel, seed, and chop tomatoes; how to chop and slice onions; how to roast, peel, and seed bell peppers; how to core, seed, and dice fresh chili peppers; how to make chicken, fish, and beef or veal stock – these are all fully explained.

The desserts cover important basics such as making pastry crusts, baking sponge cakes, toasting nuts, whipping cream, and making caramel.

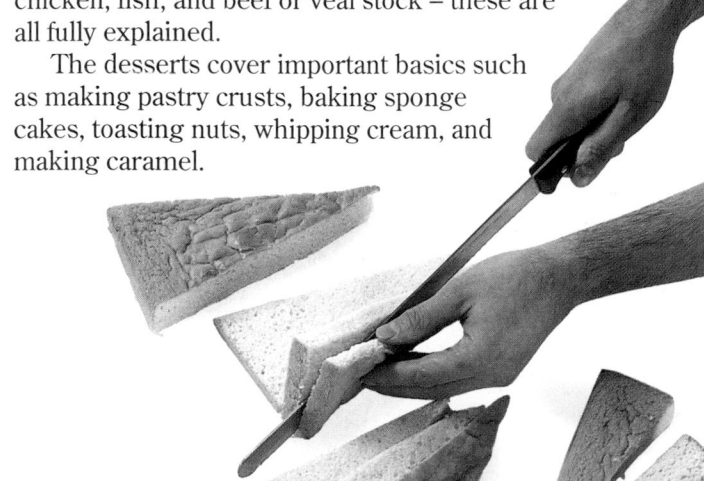

HOW-TO BOXES

In each of the recipes in **Italian Country Cooking** *you'll find pictures of all the techniques used. However, some basic preparations appear in a number of recipes, and they are shown in extra detail in these special "how-to" boxes:*

INDEX

ACKNOWLEDGMENTS

*Photographer*s David Murray
Jules Selmes
Photographer's Assistant Ian Boddy

Chef Eric Treuille
Cookery Consultants Martha Holmberg
Annie Nichols
Home Economist Sarah Lowman

US Editor Jeanette Mall

Typesetting Linda Parker
Text film by Disc to Print (UK) Limited

Production Consultant Lorraine Baird

*Anne Willan owes special thanks to
consultant Henry Grossi for his
invaluable guidance on Italian
recipes and cooking techniques.*

*She would also like to thank her chief
editor Kate Krader and associate
editors Stacy Toporoff and Jacqueline
Bobrow, together with Cynthia Nims,
for their vital help with writing this
book and researching and testing the
recipes, aided by La Varenne's chefs
and trainees.*